MW00681290

Hard Road Home

ISBN 978-0-9816989-4-6
Library of Congress Control Number: 2013956256

Copyright © 2014 Ragged Banner Press
All rights reserved.

Front cover central image:
  Detail from a photograph by Lang Ching-shan.

Printed in the United States of America on alkaline paper.

Ragged Banner Press
P.O. Box 471
Dobbs Ferry, NY 10522
USA

http://www.raggedbanner.com

Hard Road Home

Selected essays

by

Ye Fu

Translated from the Chinese by A. E. Clark

Ragged Banner Press
Dobbs Ferry, New York

CONTENTS

PREFACE

*'Venisti tandem, tuaque exspectata parenti
vicit iter durum pietas?'*

Aeneid VI.687-8

An arduous journey drives the classical epic, and the protagonist's goal is often an apparently modest one: to recover his place and reëstablish his roots. But monsters and spiteful deities beset the hero homeward bound: only after ten years and the death of all his companions does Odysseus reach Ithaca, where he finds scoundrels giving orders in his house. Aeneas suffers likewise en route to his new homeland; and once he strays into a dark wood, Dante's only way back is a path through Hell. Sorely tried, each of them visits the underworld seeking counsel from the dead. It's a hard road that takes them home.

In the West, faith in Progress undermined this metaphor: it grew difficult to imagine heroic journeys moving in any other direction than forward. But in China, the ancestral home and the spirits of one's forebears long retained a numinous power. Even today, some Chinese sense that to resolve an existential crisis one may need to go back—not to restore the past, but to remember it truthfully and draw strength from the good in it. The pursuit of hard memories without

i

easy answers typically arouses psychological resistance. In China, there are two external obstacles as well: three decades of blistering economic development have left few traces of the past, and the authorities either deter or suppress discussions that could cast doubt on their legitimacy. The road back, if it can be found, is often closed.

Yet some are undeterred. These essays, which Zheng Shiping penned under the name 'Ye Fu' (The Wild Man), document such a journey of the mind and heart. In youth he knew little of his family history and only partly understood his parents' reticence. But later, he needed to know; shaken by loss and misfortune, he ventured into the desolate hills south of the Qing River to discover a past which his father had been unable to face. He came to better understand both his family and his country, whose fates had been intertwined. Though his accounts of China's epoch of war and revolution and convulsive tyranny can be harrowing, Ye Fu seeks to illuminate, not to emote or to shock. Much of his elegy for his grandfather is devoted to an *analysis* of the Machiavellian calculus that demanded a wave of violence in which more than a million landholders perished. He wants to identify the inhumane values that sprang from and sustained a regime of power without accountability. In the essay placed at the center of this collection, "An Education in Cruelty," he finds that despite all the changes China has undergone since Mao's death, those toxic values are still in play. The bureaucratic indifference and harassment which he encountered when his mother "went missing in her homeland" (p. 13) are not the same as the rampages of an earlier era, but in Ye Fu's eyes they spring from the same soil.

The reader willing to accompany the author through this bleak landscape will be rewarded with the character portraits he paints along the way. At the end, when he has helped Cheng Fenglin to make her final journey home, Ye Fu says he has written her story to pay a debt of kindness. The reader may feel he has accomplished more than that. The characters depicted in these pages are real—that is, flawed—human beings, yet though they were poor and unknown and left no mark on the maelstrom of their age, they shine with a fidelity and a loving endurance that are not easily forgotten. Perhaps they are evoked to rebuke the society that has come after them, where wealth accumulates, and men decay.

For to Ye Fu, these great souls are his country's hope. He hints that his nation as a whole needs to retrace its steps further and draw water from an ancient well. Of "the traditional culture," which "breathed decency and integrity," he says, "We threw it all away, and it won't be easy to get it back" (p. 68–69). "If we want to regain the bedrock of human nature, we still have a long way to go" (p. 60). If at times he seems to idealize China's traditional culture—a fondness reflected in his writing style, which in the original is highly literary and occasionally archaic—he never slips into a delusive nostalgia. He takes as his touchstone of goodness not culturally specific traits, but human character itself.

These notes from his journey therefore speak to a question that is on China's mind: in what does greatness consist? Does it lie in the gigantism of the state, savored vicariously by the powerless? Or in tokens of wealth and celebrity which many aspire to, and some can obtain? The commercial success of *Tiny Times* and the ongoing promotion of Xi Jinping's China Dream suggest that each of those visions exerts wide influence. These essays locate greatness elsewhere: among the broken tablets of the House of Li, and on a barren hillside hoed in famine, and in a modern hermit's quirky renunciation.

To enter his father's house, Telemachus may need to pick his way past Ferraris parked carelessly on the lawn, and the returning hero himself may be dismayed to find a huge portrait of Polyphemus exalted in the central square. But those who have made this journey affirm: *that which we are, we are.* If ever they forgot, the shades of their mothers and fathers whispered a reminder. Read on.

A. E. Clark
November 2, 2013
Dobbs Ferry

ACKNOWLEDGMENTS

The generous and patient assistance of a few Chinese friends made this translation possible. *A.* helped me read most of these essays and explained many of their details, after *P.* had suggested I translate some of these pieces and contacted the author on my behalf. *F.* advised, as did Han-ping Chin. *L.* clarified difficult passages. Zemin Zhang helped me read two of the essays, solved many problems, and offered kind encouragement.

Joy Jia-Wan Teng suggested valuable corrections after comparing drafts of the translations to the original texts. Further corrections were provided by Paul Windels III, Peggy Sweeney, and Han-ping Chin.

Ye Fu graciously answered many questions, shared old photographs of his family, and bore with delays.

Ellen Hurley Clark and Johanna Clark walked with me along this road.

Deficiencies that remain are no one's fault but mine.

A.E.C.

Hard Road Home

This volume is dedicated to the souls
of my maternal grandmother
and my father and mother.

Cheng Kelan, née Liu Lingyun, *circa* 1950.

A Mother to the River Gone

On the tenth anniversary of my mother's disappearance

This essay lingered in my mind a long time before I found the courage to write it. It was strung so taut I feared it would snap with a twang at the lightest touch. Nay, call it a stone upon my throat, all through the sleepless nights: in the darkness, a rending grief. One quiet memory was enough to shatter whatever complacency I had wrought for myself as a sojourner in this world.

Fall has returned, south of the Yangtze, and the cool rises from the autumn waves as winter gathers strength. It's been exactly ten years, but I—a migrant in the North—still can't bring myself to revisit those ice-cold waters where my mother jumped, nor do I want to imagine where she may yet lie unburied in moonlight.

ଏ

Considering the uncompromising personality which she retained into her old age, I think it was inevitable that she would be labeled a Rightist.[1] I say this not out of a belief in Fate, but because there was etched into her being, from birth, the mark of her father. All her life she struggled to cut the ties of blood that bound her to that ranking officer of the Republic, but she could not.

My grandmother had been born into a wealthy and influential family in the alluvial plain between the Yangtze and the Han rivers. In the early period of the Republic, her father had studied for eight years in Japan. On coming home, before taking up the judgeship in Gansu to which he'd been assigned, he decided to use the marriage of his daughter to form a relationship with the Liu family that was prominent in Tianmen. The third son in that household (my maternal grandfather) was then just beginning a career in the military: he was a student slated to become an NCO in the eighth graduating class at Whampoa.[2] After perhaps a brief period of happiness, my grandmother (with my mother in tow) entered the lonely life of a soldier's wife in a time crowded with the disasters of war.

At the outbreak of hostilities with Japan, my grandfather (serving under General Chiang) withdrew to the Southwest. My great-grandfather Liu passed away, and the great house became poorer with each passing day. Back and forth through this district surged the Japanese invaders, the Army of the Republic, and the Communist forces: and with each turn in the fighting, the erstwhile manor of the Liu family was plundered anew. My grandmother took my mother, then a girl, from one hiding place to another, and they drank the refugee's cup of bitterness to the lees. Finally, to shield her daughter from dishonor, she thought it best to ask a traveling salesman to take my mother into western Hunan to shelter at an uncle's house. She found no warm reception: they worked her like a scullion, but she continued her schooling.

☙

In the year of Japan's surrender, my mother made an arduous journey to her native place in search of her mother, whom she found picking cotton and spinning it at home to eke out a living. When they met, their ragged garments were soon damp with tears. The following year, word spread among the locals that Grandfather had returned home after making good, and that he was now a major-general stationed at Wuhan. When my mother went there in search of her father, staggering news awaited her: doubting his wife and daughter could have survived, he had remarried and now had other children. What's more, he had concealed his marital history and wasn't going to acknowledge his first family now. Heartbroken and furious, my mother burst into one of his sumptuous cocktail parties and caused a scene. My grandfather went out to his hometown and forced my grandmother to agree to a divorce, which led to complete estrangement between father and daughter: to seal the rupture, my mother changed her name.

Ever-turning are the ways of Heaven: after a string of defeats, in 1948 my grandfather received orders transferring him to Enshi.[3] Ambushed en route, he took a bullet in the chest. The person who showed up to manage the funeral and walk behind his coffin was my grandmother, who would live the rest of her life as a widow.

The following year power changed hands in Wuhan and "Revolution U." began admitting students.[4] My mother passed the exam and at the completion of her studies she was dispatched, by a curious coincidence, to Enshi to help with counterinsurgency and land reform. She took the same route on which her father had perished. On this dangerous mountain road, she happened to meet my father. She, a general's daughter left behind on the plains and now orphaned; he, the heir of a Tujia chieftain of declining fortunes in the hill-country; in that era of vast unrest, some mixture of fate and coincidence led these two to marry and put down roots in the remote mountains.

∽

My grandmother had long since forgiven her husband, but my mother harbored an undying hatred for the man. She had no way to punish him in reality but strove for retribution in her mind. She changed her name (both first and last), never acknowledged that she'd had this man as her father, and even resented her mother's clemency.

Her rebellion, however, could never amount to anything but venting, because this Party of ours has always put much store by bloodlines as signaling membership in one or another class. From the day she registered at Revolution U., she had to fill out innumerable forms. She always tried to explain that she'd been abandoned in infancy by her father and his class, that she and her mother belonged to the common people in their hardships. But these forms gave little space for explanation, and of their limited selection of ready-made labels, one stuck to her.

There was a phrase much-used in the last century that had fatal implications: "History unclear." This little phrase caught her in an unbearable vise. When someone had a problem with her and pressed the question, "Are you or are you not the daughter of a warlord?" she was in a bind. She hated her father more than they did, but they still identified her with him as part of the same enemy. When alive, this father had abandoned her; dead, he brought her no end of harm. It was a quagmire, this consanguinity, from which she could never escape.

In 1957, Mother was thirty and ought to have felt established in her life. She had tried so hard to transplant her well-bred ways from the provincial capital to that mountain settlement of the Tujia! But her good intentions, often bluntly expressed, met with ill-will. When people drew a connection between her background and some offhand comments she made about the Party, there could be only one outcome: she was labeled a Rightist and sentenced to Reform under Workers' Supervision. Twenty years later her name was cleared in a full rehabilitation, but by then she'd grown old, and who was going to make restitution for all the indignities and injuries she had suffered? Condemnation and rehabilitation are each, basically, just a piece of paper: but to my mother the first was as heavy as a mountain, and the second as light as a feather.

෴

With the Cultural Revolution, my father—being the director of a mine—was quickly knocked down,[5] and my mother's meager wages had to keep the whole family alive. In those days she was employed at the town's grocery cooperative as a skilled bookkeeper (she could work the abacus with both hands). When schools were closed and my eldest sister was sent to an agricultural production brigade on the plains, Grandmother went with her. Second Sister toiled in the mines. My father, now critically ill, was hospitalized in Wuhan, and I was in precarious condition at ten years old, for my lungs were riddled with tuberculosis. Our family, separated four ways, entered its time of maximum danger. All the same, people kept writing big-character posters attacking my mother and plastered them on our windows and door, and our home was the target of frequent raids that took away even our sewing machine. But Mother, focused on the tasks before her, endured all these humiliations. She brought me into town to seek medicine and doctoring; she was resolved to haul her shattered family into an uncertain tomorrow and lose no one along the way.

On one occasion she had taken me to the county seat for medical care and asked an acquaintance to arrange a ride home. When the driver passed outside the city limits, he stopped and ordered us out of the cab of his truck. And my mother, who had never bowed her head to anyone, pleaded with him piteously for my sake; and watching with rage and grief as the vehicle sped off in a cloud of dust, she still would not let her son see his mother hard-pressed and embarrassed. There was nothing for it but to swallow her tears once again. She could never understand how the malice of this world of men could go so far, how in a single generation human nature became so horribly warped.

When I finished the elementary grades, the school authorities refused to register me for middle school on the grounds that I had a communicable disease, and for a while I became a teenaged woodcutter. When I tottered home after sundown shouldering a bundle of faggots and my mother, now haggard, came out to meet me with her unkempt hair blowing in the wind, who could have guessed she had been a child of privilege? My sisters had both had their education cut short; she wasn't going to let me, too, slip into the mire. She felt impelled to go see the local education officials and eventually had me cleared to enter school.

ᛯ

Thus did she shepherd our whole family into 1978, a year of welcome changes.[6] Father was promoted; Mother was re-habilitated; my older sister found a regular job; I passed the college entrance exam; and Grandmother came back to live with us. In these days Mother once again wore a smile and dared to believe that decency, in the end, will be rewarded. When people who had persecuted her dropped by our house, she received them without strain.

Grandmother died in 1983 and in 1985 my parents re-tired with honor. In '87 my father developed cancer; in '89 I resigned from law enforcement and soon afterward went to prison;[7] thus began the grim twilight of my mother's life. Re-solved to hold on at least till his boy returned to the sunlight, my father submitted to extremely painful surgeries—some-times two in the same year. Parts of his body were excised one after another, till little was left but his tenacious will to live. It was even harsher for my mother, who drove herself relentlessly as she took my father to the provincial capital for care. Though in her sixties, she would unroll a mat on the floor beside his hospital bed and keep watch through

Zheng Yonghuai and Cheng Kelan, *circa* 1993
(The author's parents)

his troubled nights and days. When he was ambulatory, she would escort him on visits to the prison, and the three of us saying farewell at the iron gate made for a sorry sight at which even the guards were moved. We waved goodbye each time as if it was forever; and these two stooped elders, who had given so much to their country, had to face in their last days the shame of the high wall and the electrified fence. During spells when we couldn't meet, we maintained frequent correspondence, and my mother would always add a few pages to my father's long dense missives. In those days I was in a bind: I hoped that my father and I would see each other again in this life, but I also wanted him to let go. His struggle was too bitter; it was dragging my mother toward the abyss.

❧

In 1995 when I went back to my old home in the hill country, Mother dwelt alone in the empty house, gathering oddments of cloth to sew. Father had been dead for just half a year. Atop the roof he had planted a prickly ash tree[8] and it had taken root in a slightly miraculous fashion. Now it was in full bloom, its countless blossoms wide-open like the eyes of those who die awaiting vindication. As if it were the same old me, merely returned from a bit of wandering, Mother stir-fried some chicken giblets and cabbage and then brought out a jug of medicinal wine: "Drink. Your Dad brewed this for you: it cures the damage done by overwork." Perhaps she couldn't know that her son's wounds were in his soul, but she hoped this old remedy would bring him

9

comfort. To make a living, I had no choice but to leave the hill country at once. At my departure, something came over Mother and she tugged at my hand. "Once you're settled in Wuhan, take me in to live with you, OK? The house is so empty now. It spooks me being here alone." I felt then that Mother had grown old indeed; nothing was left of the staunch fearlessness that had borne her through life. All of a sudden, she was like a child who's afraid to be left alone.

✑

With money borrowed from friends, I rented a filthy room with a few pieces of rickety furniture that allowed me to call it a home. Mother brought a single-door refrigerator whose many nicks and scratches had been touched up with paint—a melancholy sight, for this appliance was the only property of any value that remained at the end of two old people's frugal lives: the disasters of this transitory existence had used up everything they had. What could I possibly do for her to make it right?

In the dim room, Mother set about unraveling her woolen sweater. She washed the crimped strands of yarn and then knitted for me, stitch by stitch, a pair of trousers. "It's not easy to buy this good old-fashioned wool anymore. You wear this, it'll keep you warm."

She brought out a lot of writing paper which she'd bound into a big book for me. It was a family chronicle she'd written in the last few years. I saw tens of thousands of characters penned in a small dense hand, and almost every page sported a blot or two from tearstains. Her hands shook a little and she choked up as she gave it to me. "This will have to do as an heirloom for you three kids."

She stopped cooking, she who had always cooked for me, and now each day she wouldn't eat till I came home and cooked something. She said the house was gloomy and cold during the day and filled her with a kind of dread. I took her to the Neighborhood Committee where she could play mahjong; she went once, but wouldn't go again, saying she had nothing to talk about with those old people. I realized that, with her refined sensibility, my mother had steered clear of dull conventionalities all her life and would never find pleasure in them.

At that time I'd scraped together a little money with my friends to start a publishing venture. Each day when I came home, Mother would ask whether we'd made any money, and I'd say business wasn't like that, things don't happen so fast. She would sigh that prices kept going up and it was awfully expensive to live in the city. Then she said if she fell ill she'd be a burden to us; she had a mind to join my father. As this cold, indifferent world ran me ragged, day after day, I asked a friend's wife to give Mother some free medicine because her heart was starting to ail her. "Mom," I said, "Everything's going to get better."

❧

After two weeks, Mother asked to go live with my oldest sister. My sister had an apartment of narrow rooms in a different part of the same city, beside the Yangtze. And she had a sweet little girl who I thought might lift Mother's spirits a bit and be a comfort to her. So I agreed, and my sister came and took her.

Still struggling to make my way in the world and at that time lacking a phone, I was careless about staying in touch. Actually, the problem was I had failed to recognize the hints Mother had dropped and I didn't know she had made up her mind to go. She was already planning her funeral in her mind and, in a roundabout way, was saying goodbye.

One afternoon in the late autumn of 1995, my sister phoned a friend of mine, trying to reach me. Mother had gone out in the morning, she said, and still hadn't returned; they'd looked everywhere without finding her. There was an edge of panic in my sister's voice. Still, I said, "It won't be anything too serious; you all keep looking." At nightfall she phoned again, sobbing. My mother had left a note.

I hurried over with some friends and she handed me two letters which had been found hidden under the bedclothes. There was also a set of keys and, on the keyring, the filigreed gold ring which Father had given her long ago. My heart froze.

Mother had written calmly:

I know I'm sick, now, and I've been dreaming that my mother is calling me. I took care of your father to the end, and I waited for Ping'r[9] to come back: at last my work is done. I want to go see your father. Please forgive me. I've gone to the Yangtze; don't look for me, you won't find me. The three of you need to help each other out, your parents weren't able to leave you anything, and if I don't go, I'll just be a burden to you . . .

☙

We searched along the river all night, hoping that Mother still wavered at the edge of life, that there was still one last chance.

When we reported it to Public Security, they said it would be enough to come back a month after the individual's disappearance; the file could be prepared then. When we asked for help at the Bureau of Civil Affairs, they said they weren't responsible for finding missing persons. When we went to the TV station, they said the management didn't let them broadcast appeals about missing persons because there were just too many of them. We photocopied some posters and started plastering them all over the streets; the Code Enforcers tore them down and when they caught us, fined us.[10] In all our country, there wasn't a single office or aid organization willing to get involved; and thus my mother went missing in her homeland.

Longshoremen know much about the river and its ways. They told me that Yangluo, downstream from Wuhan, was a backwater of the Yangtze and that the floating bodies of the drowned tended to collect there.[11] That's where you should look for your mother, they said.

So I went alone to Yangluo Town and rented a room on the waterfront and sought help at the police station-house. They were polite. "You see how many Missing notices there are on this wall? We couldn't possibly keep up with them. New bodies float in every day. There used to be a farmer who'd retrieve the bodies and bury them; we gave him a hundred yuan for each one and recorded the particulars. But the budget's itemized, now: we don't have any discretionary funds for that sort of thing. Rent a small boat yourself, and go and look."

I found a fisherman who had no qualms about rowing me out in his skiff every day to linger and crisscross at this bend in the river. As predicted, corpses floated in each day, and I had to approach each one and check whether it was my mother. Some were rolled right up onto the beach along with the spindrift, and they'd swell and decompose in the sun, covered with flies, and the stench traveled far. But I was afraid my mother might slip by unrecognized, so I'd always go and turn over the body. After many days the fisherman wearied of this, but the longshoremen were touched by my filial piety and offered one more piece of advice. They said to quit searching. In their experience, anyone who'd fallen into the water at Wuhan should have turned up by now, and the fact that she hadn't could only mean she'd gotten snagged near the bottom on a ship's anchor or been swept past this bend, and in that case she'd never be found. All the same, I stayed in sight of the riverbank when I returned to Wuhan, but I saw no trace of Mother. During this time my sisters had been searching among relatives, friends, even temples where she might have taken refuge. Eventually we gave up hope.

໑

A full ten years have passed, and many an autumn sky has lent the cool waters its luminance, but for my sisters and me there has been no healing of grief and guilt. When we gather, we mostly avoid speaking of this, since everyone knows what hidden wounds still bleed inside.

My two sisters grew up without much education and are still somewhat superstitious, and for a few years, whenever they heard of some guru or seer they would spend their money to ask Mother's whereabouts and then follow the putative sage's directions on a futile quest. Or when neighbors reported sighting an old person who resembled Mother, my sisters would make inquiries that only renewed their grief. I alone had resigned myself to her being really gone. I knew the determination and the earnest tenderness for us which had defined her life and which, in that insuperable hour, had indeed enabled her to walk to her death unhurried and with dignity. I am convinced that she meant for her drowning to wake me up and set me back once more upon my road, to give me a future free and clear. Sixty-eight years old, at the end of a rough life, on that morning in late autumn she set her face toward the Yangtze. The water would have been as cold as a blade, then, and the rising sun blood-red; I'm not sure how to picture her, maybe glancing back as she drew near to the stream that flowed mighty and ageless. I wonder if there were tears in her eyes, the last time she looked back; I wonder if anxiety still gnawed at her for her children who had sunk into penury and disgrace. She scattered her motherly love upon the waves and surrendered her worn-out flesh as nourishment for the fish[12]—what steadfastness, what benevolence! The leap itself could not have been easy for her; a splash parted the quiet waters, and the ripples rock my mind to this day.

In the winter of 1995, I built for her a small cenotaph, and beside it I buried Grandmother's remains and Father's ashes. Then I set out on my journey, from which there would be no turning back.

A year later I read "Kaddish," Allen Ginsberg's long poem in memory of his mother, when I was editing a book on the Beat Generation. Ginsberg keeps coming back to the last letter his mother wrote him before she died:

> *The key is on the windowsill, the key is in the sunlight at*
> *the window.*
> *My child, get married, don't smoke dope.*
> *The key is in the sunlight . . .* [13]

I was in Beijing's Purple Bamboo Park on a moonlit night in early spring when I read this, and the lines made me weep as though a century of tears, long dammed, had broken through. For I, too, could now see the key that my mother had left for me in the sunlight . . .

The Watcher at Great Well

When talk turns to Great Well, that scenic landmark in the district I hail from, my first thought is always of an old man rambling through the ancient stronghold alone in the crimson glow of sunset.[14] His figure was short and somber, yet I feel now that the vast courtyard and gabled roof of the Li clan's ancestral hall provided the setting for *his* life, the stage on which *his* tragedy played out from beginning to end.[15] Today Great Well is world-famous, but that man perished in obscurity—I can't even find out when he died—and those hooded eyes are closed forever. I don't think anyone else has cherished his memory as I have. But perhaps a few old folks are left whose recollections will be stirred by my tale.

Twenty years ago when I was an idle functionary in the bureaucracy of Lichuan, my Department Chief gave me leave to explore the city's environs in order to complete a volume devoted to the folk history of Lichuan.[16] My peregrinations brought me to Great Well. Thanks to lessons in Class Struggle I'd received in my youth, I had certainly heard of the place (as an object-lesson, it ranked up there with the manor of Liu Wencai[17]); but the first time I visited this jewel of a building I was astounded. Deep in the Ba mountain range that runs between two provinces, in a stretch of bleak and undeveloped land, one suddenly encounters this colossal and classically elegant edifice—it is uncanny.

At that time, the area around Great Well still lacked a hotel and there were only a few scattered dwellings near the Manor. What passed for the local government had hung its shingle at the courtyard named "In the Shade of the Blue Lotus," but not even a mess cook was to be found; in search of a place to stay, I turned my steps toward the Hall of the Ancestors. In those days, the Hall had been put to use as a grain-distribution center and a school, but with the grain-distribution center defunct, there remained only the school, which had a wing where a few teachers lodged like ascetic monks at an ancient temple. I had once done a stint as a petty official in the Education Bureau and when I mentioned this part of my background, a young teacher warmed to me and let me have his berth in the simple dorm for a few days. I was thus able to settle into the old manor among the deserted hills and take my time looking around.

When the teachers learned why I was there, they all said that to understand the story behind Great Well and the House of Li, I need only meet Old Qiu—a solitary fellow who lived nearby. "Where?" I asked; they pointed to a thatched hut halfway up the mountainside behind the Manor. I wanted to go talk to him, but they said that was unnecessary: I could just wait for him, for at dusk he would come to fetch water.

Sure enough, toward evening Old Qiu approached with vigorous strides bearing a couple of buckets on a shoulder-pole. At a distance he seemed a perfect example of the traditional Tujia style: he was garbed in a blue robe with a sash at his waist and a black turban on his head, and his feet were shod in straw sandals.[18] I stepped forward to greet him and introduce myself, and the old man gave a little bow in response, neither subservient nor haughty, and imperturbably went about his business drawing water from the famous well. Then with two full buckets across his shoulders he climbed a flight of steps without visible strain and left the hall, taking the dirt road up the mountainside toward his thatched home. I went along, and halfway there I insisted on taking a turn with the buckets, but after a few steps I was panting like an ox and the old man reclaimed his burden. His home stood in a patch of tobacco plants halfway up the hillside, all by itself, with no living soul visible in any direction. His four walls, if they could be called that, were the roughest of lumber nailed together, and the view from his house was via the chinks in the lumber, and the whole roof was overspread with cogongrass. Inside there was a bed, a wood-burning stove, a water crock, a couple of chairs, and nothing else I can recall except bare necessities. To see the circumstances in which he lived unnerved me. He filled the crock, pulled out a creaky chair, and invited me to be seated as he fixed me some coarse tea in an old mug. Then he rolled himself a cigarette and calmly asked the reason for my visit. After I'd explained, the old man seemed lost in thought for a moment and then shook his head with a melancholy smile. "Finally . . . someone finally came to learn what happened to the House of Li."

After a pause, he brought me outside to view the ancestral hall and the Manor, explaining the principles of their layout. Then he took me back down there, and we climbed the ramparts and walked along the high wall overgrown with grass and brambles. He spoke of the past, recounting in detail the rise and fall of a great house. He must have been in his seventies, then, but he sprang upon ramparts and scampered down steps with the agility of some martial-arts master in disguise—the effect was startling.

In his youth the old man had been captain of the guard at the Li estate, and he had trained hard in the arts of war. An expert marksman, he had more than once helped beat off the attacks of marauding cultists, local bandits, or troops serving the warlord of that region.[19] The last scion of the family, Li Gaiwu, trusted him completely. At the outbreak of the War of Resistance against the Japanese, Li Gaiwu put him in command of a company of infantry that marched to Yichang and took part in the battle there.[20] He wore the insignia of a Captain in the Army of the Republic. After the victory over Japan, he retired from the service and returned home to find that his wife had gone off with another man, taking their only daughter with her; he divorced her and lived alone from then on, for his daughter married and settled in Enshi.

The old man brought me back into the main hall and expounded on the distinctive features of the Manor's construction. He pointed to one of the columns supporting the roof beams: "Look: each of the other columns is centered on the stone base beneath it, but this one is off-center. Back in the 1940s, a kung fu master named Wan Laiming was passing through Fengjie and when he dropped by to pay his respects to Li Gaiwu, he gave an extemporaneous kung fu demonstration in this very hall. First he took off his outer garments and, using the grappling technique called 'Uprooting the Willow,' he lifted this pillar off its base and slipped his clothes underneath. At the close of his demonstration, he lifted the pillar again and retrieved his clothes, but when he put the pillar down this time it was slightly off-center." The old man told me he had been present, and at the lifting of the pillar he'd heard a cracking sound among the shingles on the roof, but no damage had been done. Everyone had marveled at Master Wan's prodigious feat. Today you can still see the irregularity in that column. Considering all he'd been through, Old Qiu was a low-key and unpretentious man. Although I have trouble crediting that kung fu master with such superhuman power, Qiu didn't seem to be telling tall tales and I have decided after some hesitation to include this anecdote.

The old fellow had a deep attachment to his former master and when he recounted how Li Gaiwu met his end, one could not miss the deep grief that welled up in him. He said that at the time when power in the country was changing hands, Li—a local squire—saw the writing on the wall and swiftly reached out to the new government. During the insurrection that followed (the so-called "bandits' rebellion"), the rebels made overtures to him, but he instructed Qiu and his other retainers not to respond and he even notified the new government secretly about these developments, and for this the new government in Fengjie would later commend him.

But during the land-reform campaigns that followed the imposition of peace across the nation, Li Gaiwu was seized as a local despot by peasants who'd been riled up during the campaigns, and they roasted him alive over an open flame.[21] This atrocity, the impulsive act of a mob, was never documented in any official record. Although the tale originated in eyewitness accounts, there is probably no longer any way to verify it. But considering all the cruelty and all the travesties of justice wrought by succeeding generations, I'm inclined to believe it. In the wake of a great revolutionary era when it became normal for the lower strata to hate the rich, and it was perfectly legal to plunder them, evil passions could easily have been fanned into that barbaric flame. When Old Qiu turned to me in the enveloping twilight and huskily recounted the clan's agony, there stole over me an unspeakable dread of this mansion, so ornate and festooned with cobwebs. I distinctly felt a burning pain on my skin—oh, the torment that must have been!

In one night a large clan and the estate which it had taken generations to build collapsed forever. Among all the area's inhabitants, there was scarcely to be found a single descendant of the House of Li. I found this horrifying. It was as if a long-standing nest had been poked apart, leaving eggs broken and scattered on the ground; the swallows have flown and the people are gone, never to return. But Old Qiu stayed behind, this lonely man who had no one to count on, whose only livelihood had been the arts of war. He was branded a bad element in one campaign after another,[22] yet he somehow managed to survive till the '80s. Once a skilled warrior, after the annihilation of the House of Li he kept watch by the ancestral hall whose sun had set, like some faithful servant of ancient times remaining at his master's grave. Almost daily he came to the Hall's courtyard just to hang around, continuing to draw from the immemorial well the water that sustained him, and in its reflection he saw Time's changing face. No matter how much water he bore away on his shoulders, the well never ran dry, like an eye filled with pain whose tears flow unceasing. Cold water his only drink and a gourd his rice-bowl, he grew old keeping watch to no purpose and aged into a wraith. Of his former prosperity and honor nothing remained but a wry memory; when every day he stopped in his pacing at the edge of the ramparts, where the moaning wind caressed his face, was he remembering his own age of heroism, of steed and blade? Did he feel duty-bound, still, to defend with his life the last redoubt?

I stayed a few more days, and the two of us became friends despite the difference in our ages. He took me into a few peasants' homes to show me broken stone tablets on the ground and pieces of old furniture that had come from the Manor. He even pulled open the drawers of a few tables to reveal inscriptions engraved with golden characters—for the drawers had been made from fragments of plaques that bore the Li clan's family precepts. In the dusky room, gilt characters gleamed with the radiance of an era that could never be put back together again. All these relics bore the scuffs and dents of time: the ashes of a vanished ascendancy for which he alone still grieved.

Under towering crags, this land abides in beauty;
Imbued with the classics, its race preserves honor and justice.

The two lines of this couplet hung at opposite ends of the ramparts next to the ancestral hall. The mountains still towered as before, but neither the classics nor the honor and justice that had flowed from them were much in evidence. The family had long since ceased preserving anything, including themselves. All that remained was this deserted hall on the vast and untrammeled borderland between Hubei and Chongqing, an ancient marvel inspiring reverence for our history. To this day I remember the moonlight on the mountains. I can see the silhouette of Old Qiu receding into the distance like some lost soul emblematic of an age, and the image leaves me at a loss for words.

On the morning of my departure, he came to see me off at the village gateway. I had bought some boiled eggs for him, which he accepted, but to a small sum I offered as well he made a dignified refusal. When the country bus took me away, it was the first of many stages that led me back into the outer world. But afterward whenever I had guests from that district, I would ask quietly for news of Old Qiu. In this way I eventually learned that the old man had died somewhile, and I realized that the last of the insiders of that mighty House was gone. For more than eighty years, he had clung fast to the Manor, but in the end he could take none of it with him, not even the smallest tile. His lifework finished, he had found himself in an era that had no respect for anything. And so there *was* still something for him to guard: a secret about this world of men that he glimpsed before going home to the eternal silence.

Recently the ancestral hall of the House of Li was designated a National Treasure, but I have to wonder whether any of the officials buzzing back and forth ever knew the old man's story. Perhaps the rise and fall of fortunes in this world of dust can only be seen, as if reflected in a bronze mirror, at that ancient spring-fed well when its jade depths shimmer with moonlight.

Requiem for a Landlord

A Chronicle of Land Reform
and the Destruction of a Family

No matter what his reason—shame, embarrassment, fear, or some other painful emotion—it's hard for me to understand why my father avoided for so long any mention of his parents and siblings. Even in the placid latter part of his life he could not be drawn to reminisce as most old folks love to do. Like a blind traveler who skirts the pitfalls along a familiar route, he steered clear of that buried epoch. One could get the impression he had arrived on this planet like a meteorite; behind him lay an immense void. There were no traces of the path by which he'd come, only an enigmatic nebula in the depths of space.

In consequence, the stream of my lineage could be traced back only as far as my father's generation; beyond that, it went dry. I myself was like a rivulet with no fountainhead, which the parched ground will soak up as it spreads out. Yet this is illogical. No matter how inaccessible the existence of my paternal grandparents (as if they were legends), I think both my father and I had as our very foundation the ruins of his extensive clan. For it was that which, locked away for years like an unfathomable dream-image, quietly gave each of us the strength to survive upon this bitter earth.

It was after he died that I got a glimpse of my father's family history. In the winter of 1994, I hurried with a police escort to the funeral in Enshi. Father seemed at peace, now, laid out beneath a blood-red Party flag, bearing with him the enormous secret under whose weight he had suffered his whole life, and awaiting the fire at the end of it all. It was as if he had decided to take all the desolation in his heart and burn it to cinders. His deathbed wish—the only one—was that his ashes be scattered on the Qing River, so that the stream might bear him back to his ancestral home.

Ancestral home? Really? We'd never been there; did we even *have* an ancestral home? Yet from that ancestral home there now arrived a great many relatives, shabbily dressed; they called me "uncle" or other terms of kinship. Those of my generation were all much older than I; it left me dumbfounded, this throng of far-off relatives who had suddenly come out of the woodwork. I'd always assumed my father had neither an ancestral home nor kinsfolk, since—though a modestly successful official—he had never gone back and never mentioned them. I and my siblings had judged it tactful not to inquire. These strange clansmen who came from deep in the hill country shared my grief, and as they sobbed in mourning by my side, they began to reveal to me our family's unhappy past.

☙

Badong is perhaps the most ancient named settlement in western Hubei. The *Commentary on the Waterways Classic* says:

> *Of the Three Gorges, long is the Wu at Badong;*
> *The threefold cry of the monkeys will move you to tears.*[23]

From this it would seem Badong has been known for a long time as one of China's places of sorrow. Here lies the district of my forefathers, behind the Three Gorges, in the hinterland of the Ba mountain range. To this day it remains isolated, impoverished, and barren.

As its name implies, it is the territory of the Ba people, a wilderness that even in remote antiquity had lost its national identity. Under the Qing, it came under the jurisdiction of the Rongmei chieftain; in the nation that was pleased to call itself a republic, its precise designation was Hubei Province, Badong County, Willow-Pond District, Sijing Commune, Flagstone Squad. Now it has been incorporated into Jinguoping Town, which happens to be the site of one of the Communist Party's first martyrs, one Duan Dechang who was murdered by a fellow-official.

My grandfather's home was eight *li* from Flagstone Village, halfway up the mountain.[24] Even today, there are no signs of habitation within two *li* of his home. If you look over the cliff behind his old house, you can see the Qing River at the bottom of the 500-meter precipice, flowing swiftly as if with the tears of an inexhaustible sorrow. The village has no rice paddies. The only crops that can be planted there, where the ground's all slanted and barren, are corn and potatoes: these are the staples of the hill country. One can imagine how wild and desolate it must have been, fifty years ago. Back then it was a three days' journey to reach either the county town or the seat of the prefectural government. They knew naught of the Han, still less of the Wei and Jin.[25] They depended for their livelihood entirely on the heavens' gift of rain. If the weather were mild, most would harvest a bushel or two, enabling them to pay the Emperor's grain tax with enough left over to live in peace and self-sufficiency. They knew no -isms, put no faith in parties and factions, and didn't even care when the Government began to exercise more direct control over them.[26] They had forgotten where they came from and were vague on the distinction between the Ba and the Chu.[27] What they knew is that the larger nation in which they dwelt had always been in turmoil: all they wanted was to work hard as citizens of a world at peace.

cᴖ

Ever since China was unified under the Qin Dynasty, one could call it a great and mighty country; yet even long after the system of counties and prefectures was developed to administer it, the Central Government was in fact too far off for its authority to reach most places, and many districts remained outside the pale of Chinese civilization. Though the Imperial Court could appoint a county magistrate to a place, it was customary for him to travel there alone to take up his duties and to hire a secretary out of his own purse. As for the ethnic-minority districts, the practice was to choose a chief from a distinguished local family. This person, and his heirs, would govern the place autonomously.

In our time a county typically has more than 10,000 government employees, and paramilitary troops, police, and special agents stand ready; even so, they often request outside assistance when there's trouble. A hundred years ago, how did a county magistrate assisted by a handful of petty officials manage to dispatch all the public business and keep the peace? For the control of civil society, the Court relied on the gentry class and the village elders to take care of things without being told. Traditional decorum, as enshrined in family precepts and village ordinances passed down by generations of country squires, gave form to the Chinese people's ethical sense of how life should be organized. No matter what political and dynastic changes occurred in the distant capital, the mountain people in their forests held fast to their traditional sense of what was right. Quietly they tilled the earth and satisfied the imperial levies of men and grain, happy to lead a simple life. They were not litigious or contentious. Except in times of extreme hardship, they were unlikely to rebel.

How did the gentry class come into being? Neither by imperial appointment nor by hereditary office nor by the direct election of a grass-roots democracy. They coalesced naturally with the tacit consent of the local society. Generally speaking, this class was composed of upright, honest men who had built their families' fortunes and were well-educated and decorous. They received no salary or official title from the State. Their influence came from their personal character: when they spoke, the village listened. They might wear homespun and till the fields, but a serious word from them often sufficed to heal a division or settle a dispute. Notwithstanding the periodic upheavals in dynastic politics, society enjoyed a harmonious stability under their benevolent and watchful care. It fell to them to discharge many of the functions of government and keep the peace.

But the gentry class did not consist exclusively of a few families or a few clans. There was constant turnover. In Europe, the aristocracy followed the rule of primogeniture: their wealth, undivided down through generations, served to concentrate political power and they could better maintain their preëminence. But in China, outside the formal institutions of government, the tradition was for inheritance to branch out like a tree, and with this system of dividing family property, different branches of a family might rise or fall at different times. Hence it came to be that a family's wealth seldom lasts three generations, and no families wear the official's tasseled cap forever. Chinese society consistently encouraged people to contend as individuals: you might have been born in a rural cottage, but as long as you refrained from crime, you could toil to raise your economic status or study to pass the Imperial examinations, and then you, too, would be one of those men whom villagers saluted with respect. Refer to Lin Yaohua's classic of sociology, *The Golden Wing*, for more on this theory.[28]

Throughout history, most who ascended the Imperial throne took care to cultivate and protect the gentry class. Even the Manchu *arrivistes* dared not do away completely with the status of the gentry south of the Yangtze. For the rulers understood that this vast and populous land could not be governed solely from the barrel of a gun; among the wildflowers where their writ barely reached, they needed men of character and standing to safeguard the foundations of social order. To persecute such men represented the abandonment of the truths that had undergirded Chinese civilization for ages. And a people that has lost its fundamental truths is like a zombie without a soul: it may even degenerate into an instrument for mass murder.

❧

Migration within China during ancient times is a historical puzzle. The destinations appear wild and barren even today, and it is a mystery how our forefathers managed to discover them and develop them hundreds of years ago. Flagstone Village is situated in a region of high mountains and deep gorges along the boundaries where the three counties of Badong, Hefeng, and Jianshi meet. It's about a thousand meters above sea level, and the very name of the place hints at the hard barrenness of the soil. From the peak you can look down upon the Qing River, but it flows at the bottom of a 300-meter precipice that ensures a chronic water shortage in Flagstone. This autumn, when I visited my ancestral village for the first time, I found a cousin of mine still depending on the rainwater collected in a stone pit behind his home.

I've always thought we are descendants of Zheng Guogong, who founded one of the five primordial families of the Ba people. They are known to history as a branch of the 'barbarians with wooden shields' who liked to sing of the bamboo and the willow[29], and very possibly they are our ancestors. There is no way, after hundreds of years of staggering change, I can speak with confidence about that era. I cannot imagine, therefore, why a distant generation of my forebears sought refuge in this lonely, rugged place bereft of resources.

My honorable grandfather Zheng Zhenlüe was probably born in the first years of the Guangxu Emperor,[30] his father having been the youngest son. At the beginning of the Republican era, and perhaps even later, Grandfather's branch of the family was still quite poor, but his nephew Zheng Yongjie (the son of his eldest brother) had risen in the world and become chief in the league of thirteen townships around Willow Pond and Yesanguan. Uncle Yongjie probably enjoyed considerable distinction for that time and place: he had his own militia[31] to guard his fortified village and to this day you can see in Flagstone the ruins of the blockhouses that were part of his fortifications. The tale of He Long's assault on the Zheng compound is still told.[32] Uncle Yongjie's branch of the family never recovered after He's division smashed his stockade and massacred the defenders.

For his home, Grandfather chose a site on the mountainside eight *li* outside the village and his family dwelt alone as if in a hermitage. He raised four sons, of which my father was the youngest, and two daughters. He seems to have been more of a thinker than other peasants: recognizing that it would be hard to support his family on slash-and-burn agriculture, he began dealing in salt on the side. The mountain village was more than three hundred *li* from the county town of Badong, and thanks to the high cliffs and plunging valleys, there were scarce three yards of level ground along the whole route. The round trip took most people six days, carrying the goods on their backs the whole way; yet Grandfather is said to have managed it in three as long as he didn't run into the Red Army or brigands. One can well imagine how hard it was, how much blood and sweat it cost a simple peasant of the hills to add to his family's wealth. It's still that way, even today.

Had he not been hardworking and thrifty, it would have been exceedingly difficult for Grandfather to prosper. Only in middle age did he acquire a little land and a house. Years of backbreaking toil had enabled him to amass a property of four hectares on the mountain slopes[33] and to build a wood-frame house of about 200 square meters. In the countryside, people like him—part farmer, part trader—were considered itinerant businessmen who had seen a bit of the world and gained a knack for making a living. The land produced only corn, and what they could not eat could be made into liquor. Grandfather built a still in his house, and his fine corn liquor was soon adding a little gaiety to the hard life of the mountain folk.

ରଚ

It was probably in the 1940s that Grandfather made the transition from a poor member of the common people to a rich peasant and then a small landholder. Like many another member of the homespun gentry who had managed to improve his family's economic standing, he lived frugally, saw to everything himself, and carefully husbanded the scraps of good fortune that came to him during the lean years of that troubled time. In this decade my eldest uncle, second uncle, and younger aunt all married and started their families. Third Uncle died young and unmarried—a sad tale but a common one in the countryside, and therefore little mourned. To address the question of the young master's (that is, my father's) education, Grandfather had established a free school in the village, the first one the place had ever had, and he hired a teacher to provide instruction in the modern style. In 1946, he sent my eighteen-year-old father to the county seat to study with a master, hoping his youngest boy would complete his education and break free from the peasant-tiller status which had been their lot for generations.

It was not solely the amassing of a fortune that qualified a man to be a country squire; he had to make some contribution to the life of the village, such as financing the building of a bridge or the repair of a road, the care of the aged or the young, and he was also expected to participate in public life. Only thus could he gain dignity and honor; only on these terms would his community fully accept him. It was Grandfather's philanthropy and achievements that made him preeminent in the clan; his title had no official weight, but in that patriarchal era men like him were the bedrock of social stability, and therefore he had a symbolic authority. Not only could he assuage upsets and resolve conflicts within the clan: it often happened that outsiders (not named Zheng) would seek him out as an arbitrator. Now in every individual there is an admixture of virtue and vice; in every affair, both right and wrong; in every decision, both fairness and partiality. This was especially true in the contentions of the village, which were little more than family quarrels—and even the most honest official has a hard time satisfactorily resolving a family quarrel in which emotions have magnified some trifling dissension. In these situations it was up to Grandfather to render judgment and impose a fine, and of necessity he made enemies as well as friends this way. Thus were sown the seeds of the calamity that would later befall him—the price which almost everyone in this world pays sooner or later for blunt talk and fair dealing.

Since ancient times, the government had encouraged the village to be autonomous. It was expected to supply a certain number of soldiers and collect the grain tax, but all other services were delegated to the local society, which could stand on its own and provide for itself. In territories that the government lacked the resources to administer, this work was completely in the hands of village headmen and depended on their integrity. Only the thorniest cases were referred to the government. With little friction between the people and their officials, each stratum of society worked more effectively: this was the state of affairs the ancients called "governing by not doing."[34]

Owing to Grandfather's prestige, the county government (under the Republic) made my oldest uncle a constable (the post was roughly equivalent to today's Director of a Village Committee). In our country this was the job title that, a few years later, would be most likely to get you executed. Security was organized at the level of families, who were bound in mutual responsibility and stood as surety for each other in such tasks as suppressing bandits and keeping out thieves. The constable's role was to keep the peace and ensure that the community met its responsibilities to the national government. I am not now in a position to evaluate the constable's merits and demerits in a mountain fastness as sparsely settled and remote as Flagstone Village. I suspect the work was dull and unrewarding and that is why my oldest uncle wanted to hand the job over to his little brother who'd just come home after graduation. Fortunately—or maybe he had learned something about the world in the course of his education—my father refused, and he asked Grandfather to keep supporting him so he could go to Enshi, the seat of the prefectural government, for advanced studies. Perhaps Grandfather had heard enough news of the outside world to have a premonition of the chaos and disaster which were drawing near: he paid the money for his youngest son, of whom he was particularly fond, to go to an unfamiliar place to study. This step—perhaps it was Fate—saved my father's life.

›

In that mountain fastness where even now no bus lines run, the ancestral hall of the Zheng clan, like a setting sun, still glows with the warmth of the time before 1948. That year my father left home, never to return, as my grand-mother showered him with advice and encouragement. He was twenty years old, and he must have cast a few backward glances as he walked away. About the world beyond the hill country his head was full of illusions, and he couldn't possibly have known he'd never come back and would never get another chance to perform a son's filial duty. That morning, sunshafts laced the air that was redolent with early spring, and the whole family (with the exception of my grandfather) clustered round the departing student—the only one who'd ever done this. There was an ancient honey-locust tree by the entrance to the settlement, and the morning dew dripped audibly from its leaves.

The parting would have been a painful one and Grand-father had missed it on purpose. Alone he had climbed the hillside behind the settlement, and there where pine and bamboo mingled in a grove of flickering light and shade, the clan's burial-ground lay in silence. The grave-mounds swelled from the earth in a pleasingly irregular pattern like an informal garden. Carnations, fragrant plantain-lilies, and Traveler's Palm bloomed quietly; the tendrils of trefoil vines and morning-glories reached out like fumbling hands prompted by the mountain breeze to restrain the souls from drifting away. There were gravestones of various sizes, grayish-white and solemn like faces, mottled with moss, and the characters graven upon the stones were indistinct, as when moisture makes the ink run in an old document. A family's history in all its hardship and glory lay buried beneath this soil, and the dull green grass returned year after year to peruse it with indifference. Grandfather must have looked over this ground wreathed in the morning mist, ground which generations had gradually made their own, with the concentration of a chess master who has miscalculated and now studies a losing position for a long time, unable to find a saving move. With eyes more than sixty years old he contemplated the bas-reliefs that depicted the dead, a whole crowd of them, like a genealogy chart in the open air. It was all recorded here, a lifetime of hardship and danger of which his memory was starting to fade. On the steps before some of the sepulchres were still to be found offerings that had been left, over the years, on Tomb-Sweeping Day: a few coarse grains of corn, an open jar of wine, a withered apple. At this moment he surely would have found it incredible that he himself was going to die unburied, and that his children would be unable to light a candle, or pour a libation, or render any homage to his name.

ↄ

My eldest and second uncles had each had four children, while my two aunts had married men in Guandian Town in the neighboring county. Each of these families remained tillers of the land and passed their days in simple self-sufficiency. Grandfather hired a farmhand,[35] however, an orphaned teenager from one of the clan's families, in an arrangement that partook of the nature of an adoption. And he divided his land among his three sons, though he and Grandmother continued to farm my father's portion. This was all he had, this landlord, but in Flagstone at that time it made him stand out as a rich man.

In the year that her youngest son departed, Grandmother's lamp burned low and went out. Her early demise allowed her to enjoy honor in death, and the imposing dignity of her funeral, like the glow of a sunset, is still remembered there. The ancients said, "Long life brings many humiliations."[36] Grandmother was fortunate. Had she lived to 1951, she would have witnessed the extermination of her family.

My father was admitted to the Qing River High School located at Five Peaks in Enshi. The following year he was expelled for brawling. For a time he wandered the shingled beaches of the river towns, unsure what to do with himself; and just then the Fourth Corps under Lin Biao swept into the seat of the prefectural government. In those days wherever the Party went, it was quick to establish colleges that practiced the techniques of brainwashing developed at Yan'an and in Manchuria, so that each locality would not lack for supervisory cadres. My father, who had reached a dead end and needed a meal ticket, enrolled with the first batch of students. He quickly learned the skills requisite for "Fighting the Landlords," redistributing property, and shooting people, whereupon he was assigned to Lichuan at the start of the great drive to "eliminate the bandits[37] and oppose local despots." His old home town could not then have been reachable by post, and he must have retained many naïve ideas about the Revolution. He may well have thought that since his family had risen from poverty only recently, they ought not to be slated for harsh measures. And so he flung himself enthusiastically into the mighty stream, and in the fight to suppress the bandits he made his mark, killing and expropriating with both guns blazing. Soon he entered the Party and became the youngest District Committee Secretary.

Whether there was any contact between my father and grandfather during 1949 and 1950, whether either one received news of the other, I have never had any way to find out, because my father kept it a secret all his life. For he had learned to protect himself with silence and if there were things he was ashamed of, he hid them beneath a stoic endurance. I think many in my father's generation were men of few words. With rigid self-control they tried to forget excruciating memories, and in many cases when they grew old they had a nervous breakdown.

℆

"Nowhere under heaven is there land that does not belong to the King."[38] For Chinese, this was the earliest understanding of land ownership. In the era before there was a king, the land was held in common: you owned whatever land your clan or tribe had cleared and developed. But when kings came on the scene, they were never chosen by the people: the one who carried violence to the extreme became king and took possession of all land under heaven.

In feudal society, the sovereign might think everything belonged to the royal 'We,' and the agricultural system may in theory have lacked the concept of territory, but private ownership of farmland was recognized. This is to say that apart from the land which the Imperial Court had claimed by right of taxation, or which was cultivated by military garrisons to feed themselves,[39] or which was assigned to the holders of particular offices, all other cultivable land (both the fields and the manors) was privately owned. As long as the taxes continued to be paid at the fixed per-acre rate, the State did not interfere with whatever sales or gifts occurred between private parties except to register the change in ownership and collect a transfer fee. The Ming Dynasty encouraged people to develop virgin land and would grant the developer a three-year tax exemption on 15 *mu,*[40] and those who could handle more were not subject to any acreage limit. In the twenty-seventh year of the reign of the first Ming Emperor, an edict was issued: "Never tax those who develop virgin land." If you endured the hardships of opening up new land for agriculture, the State forbore to tax you for it. That is why, while under the Ming 11% of the farmland was State-owned, by the Qing the proportion had fallen to 4.5%.

In 1930, during the Republican era, the government carried out a large-scale census of land and population and issued China's first Land Law. This law stipulated that any land which the State nationalized became thereby the property of the whole citizenry; that if it took over private land, the State must pay for it; that mineral resources, highways, rivers and canals and lakes, places of scenic beauty or historic interest could not be privately held; but that any land to which people had legally acquired title should remain their property.

Individuals depend on the State for their survival: they need the government to provide security, order, a legal framework, and other basic protections, and therefore they must pay taxes to the State. Among Chinese, the concept of supplying the Emperor with provisions has long been accepted and needs no rationale. The forms it has taken, such as the Single-Whip Law and From Poll Tax to Land Tax, all had a mixture of advantages and shortcomings.[41]

❧

Individuals vary with respect to talent, longevity, capacity, and strength. Two families owning plots of land may plant the same seeds, but there is no guarantee they'll reap the same harvest. Natural and man-made calamities, too, tend to widen the gulf dividing men into rich and poor, and then some will need to mortgage their land, others may need to sell it, and to be sure there will be people ready to buy. All this is effected by a market economy; with regard to individual destiny, fortune and misfortune have many invisible chains of cause and effect. And so, on the same earth, there came to dwell landlords, rich peasants, middle peasants, poor peasants, and hired farmhands.

The land question is a crucial one for an agricultural people, and it has often been the impetus for a change of dynasties. "Level the playing field! The land to him who tills it!" Such have been the slogans of many a revolutionary, though there was never a revolt whose leaders knew as much hardship as the people. The dynasty might pass to a different lineage, but the system of justice would carry on as before, and it was still the lowest stratum of the people that suffered hardship.

During the Red Army era, the Party functioned essentially as a roving band of rebels. They foraged wherever they fought, and as long as the landlords' families were left something to eat you couldn't really blame the Communists for robbing them. But when they reached northern Shaanxi and acquired their own base area, it became a question of policy. Since they wanted to maintain a united front against the Japanese, they couldn't completely defy the Nationalist government and brutalize the landlords; but they also wanted to attract the support of the poor, so they had to offer something to the common people. Therefore their approach at that time was to compel the landlords to reduce rents and interest charges while the Communists levied in-kind taxes on the peasants. To cover living expenses, the soldiers themselves developed new land for farming and launched business ventures (including raising an opium crop[42]). Mao was accepting, then, of the people who were called "liberal-minded gentlemen" and made friends with some major landholders.

After victory over the Japanese, the Communist forces rapidly grew strong and the two parties were set to contend for control of the nation. For the side that was not in power and was beginning to run out of food, what they had gained by forcing the landlords to reduce their rents no longer sufficed to cover costs, so they quickly announced a policy of land reform and measures to put it into effect. Wherever they arrived, their first step was to divide the populace according to economic class. They would find support among the poor peasants and farm laborers, make an appeal to the middle peasants, isolate the rich peasants, and wipe out the landlords. The land, housing, tools, and livestock which had belonged to the latter two classes, as well as any stockpiles of grain they had set aside, would be carved up like a melon and the peasants would be presented with new deeds to the land. The advantage of this policy was that it gave the Party both a supply of food and a source of fresh troops. Fearing that government forces might return and snatch back what they considered the fruits of victory, the common people identified with the Party against the government. The Party was more attractive, for the National Army stood as a bulwark of social order and was not free to pander this way. Consequently, the government troops came under attack wherever they went.

The possibility that a landlord's holdings of real estate might be broken up was not new, and in former times of political upheaval some individuals had had little choice but to endure the loss. But everyone involved in such redistributions had been a citizen. It was accepted that each man must be left with a means of subsistence, that you couldn't take away someone else's personal property or humiliate him or take his life. In the old Chinese Soviets, plenty of the cadres even felt this way, for in the struggle against the Japanese many of the landlords had extensive ties to the Eighth-Route Army and in fact many of the senior Communist cadres were the children of landlords. But when you did not wipe the landlords out, the lower strata of the peasants grew uneasy, because when you take away someone's wealth it is natural to worry about what he may do to you someday. When Mao became aware of this problem, he harshly criticized any soft-ness and gave a green light to the most radical violence on the part of the lowest rung in society, saying that any mistakes could be corrected later. Thus began the large-scale move-ment of Land Reform. Any cadres from landlord families were stripped of their offices, and a rabble of jobless vagrants was unleashed, and all the wickedness in human nature came to the fore in one tragedy after another. Some of these I have related in other essays; the reader may also consult the fourth volume of Mao's *Selected Works* as well as recent research into the history of the Party. I am not making this up.

છ

Dynastic change fascinates Chinese because most of the time it involves warfare and bloodletting. It's a great topic of conversation for those who witness it and has furnished ma-terial for the classic stories of popular tradition. In the grand sweep of historical narration, assassins are as it were the jest-ers who provide comic interludes; as Lu Xun once said, the cruelty of a butcher can easily be turned into a joke.[43] Ordinary folk love to hear how millions of the enemy were killed and thrill to the clang of steel; as for the people whose heads wind up on pikes, who feels for them?

Abdication in primordial times is a political myth dear to Chinese intellectuals: in historical times no one dared try it.[44] One is hard-pressed to find many incidents in history like the accession of the first Song emperor, who, after donning the yellow robe, gently persuaded his former masters to resign. That political power grows from the barrel of a gun is a hard truth that was mastered by a man who liked to read the *Mirror of Governance*.[45] Still, it was quite rare for a change of dynasty (once any insurgencies had been suppressed) to be followed by a massacre of the ordinary officials who had served the previous regime. After the Manchus settled into Beijing, they had the sense to reappoint the ministers who had served the late Ming, and toward those who refused to play along, the new Qing rulers took a basically patient and tolerant approach. After all, it is not good for the smell of blood to grow too strong in a country, as any sovereign worthy of the name should know.

The success of the Xinhai Revolution[46] at first depended on nationalistic slogans about driving out the Tatars;[47] but when the Republic had been established in place of the Qing imperial family, the binding rule was to treat those people kindly (in contrast to Soviet Russia after the October Revolution, where the Tsar's whole family, women and children included, was massacred). This was the spirit of the Republic. Indeed without this leniency there could never have been any steps taken toward a genuine republic. In the American

Civil War, the rallying cry of the North was to free the slaves and unite the country. The armies fought bloody battles, but when the South surrendered, not only were the highest officers on the losing side spared, but those who had promoted the cause of secession were not treated as criminals: even slave-owners who had bankrolled the rebel army were not pursued for vengeance. This kind of national magnanimity is the prerequisite for a genuinely democratic system.

❧

It was toward the end of 1949 that power changed hands in Enshi. When the Nationalist army beat a hasty retreat, they left behind a town divested of the machinery of government, and the Communist army passing by on its way south assigned a few cadres to deal with the liberation of this rural area. For the next year, the common people of western Hubei basically lived under conditions of anarchy. Although a few perceptive observers sensed the impending storm, most hoped the turmoil was coming to an end. The majority couldn't help thinking that since the previous government hadn't been much good, the new one might bring a turn for the better.

In this year of transition, Grandfather may have felt slightly uneasy. My oldest uncle, serving as a constable, was definitely concerned. He didn't know to whom he could submit his resignation, so he just stopped working and took care of his homestead. Their consciences were clear, for they had never wronged anyone. They even imagined that with the family's youngest boy now serving in the new government, nothing too bad could happen to them.

In 1951 every county in the Enshi prefecture commenced thorough-going land reform. Informally-organized work teams were assigned to all parts of the district. To a place as poor and remote as Flagstone, only a single man was sent, a cadre by the name of Song who had come from one of the old Chinese Soviet areas in the North. He knew all the tricks of Fighting the Landlords. There were only a few dozen households in the village then, and you could see at a glance who was rich or poor, strong or weak. First he picked a few penniless and unmarried rowdies to constitute the Peasants' Assembly. He indoctrinated them a bit and promised them rewards so they would not fear to harm their fellow-villagers. Then he called together a meeting at which the class status of each family was determined. In truth, the place was so poor that almost everyone was a peasant working his own land; there weren't even any farmhands except for the orphaned kinsman my grandfather had adopted. That made Grandfather a landlord. And Eldest Uncle was nothing but a puppet of the KMT and so classed with the dregs of society.

Grandfather, it must be noted, had seen a bit of the world. He had lived through a full cycle of sixty years, and then some. Yet although he had lived under more than one regime and knew well the mutability of this human scene, he still thought that however violently power might change hands at the top, it wouldn't bring much harm to an old farmer like himself, far from the madding crowd. As for his worldly goods, let them be taken away: though a man of Chu might lose his axe, some other man of Chu would find it:[48] after all, most of the villagers were of the same family, or at least of the same clan. How could he have known that from the highest authority the word had already gone out to exterminate the landlords—not only their wealth and their status, but their very lives? For if such a large group of gentry had been allowed to survive after being stripped of their property, they would have posed a latent threat to the new regime.

∽

Historians say the ancestors of the Tujia lived chiefly by fishing and hunting; in time they came under attack by the armies of Chu that moved in from the plains, and that was when they formed their odd custom of celebrating the New Year a day early. Sharing an uncultivated region with wild animals, each household kept firearms on hand. Many have misconstrued this practice as evidence of martial ferocity, but it was only self-protection in a dangerous environment.

Now these old Tujia blunderbusses inspired the Land Reform work teams with considerable anxiety, for though scarcely lethal, they could have disfigured someone's face. To sound out the temperament of these minority people, the cadre made the confiscation of weapons his first order of business. And Grandfather's house was the first target. He had one gun and one crossbow, but even after seizing both, Comrade Song remained uneasy. He had heard about He Long's battle with Zheng Yongjie and was convinced that a good part of Yongjie's arsenal must still be hidden somewhere in Grandfather's house. He arrested the orphan Grandfather had adopted and extracted a false confession from the boy: dozens of firearms, modern rifles, had been seen in the house! Grandfather was bound and taken to the Peasants' Association, where he was suspended on ropes and beaten. There was no way he could confess where the non-existent rifles were hidden, and as the lawless punishment escalated in violence, all he could do was endure it.

This was April 1951, the early spring when a gray chill still shrouds the high hills: China was locked in an icy grip. For days on end, the few dozen inhabitants of Flagstone Village listened to a man in his sixties scream with pain. If you know anything about the history of torture in China, you can imagine the ways this experience was made worse than death. The torture room had been set up in a house belonging to a member of the Zheng clan. One night, the cadre and the militiamen had grown weary of the task and took a break, tying Grandfather to a bed. He had gone several days without food or drink, and late that night he begged the clansman whose house it was to feed him some gruel. The clansman rose and very quietly cooked him a bowl of cornmeal soup, bringing a gourd of cold water as well, and untied him so he could sup. He warned him that he'd return just before dawn to tie him up again. Grandfather could not face the dawn, for his days had become an unending night, but knowing he needed strength to kill himself, he finished this last meal in pitch darkness. Then he took the cord with which he'd been bound and tossed it over a rafter; fashioning a noose like a necktie, he put his aged head into it and cinched it tight. By the time the owner heard the sound of his feet kicking, he had left the iniquity of his ancestral village far behind.

For ages suicide was a way to die with dignity, but in the New China it has always been considered a crime, a subversive evasion of punishment. His corpse was dragged in front of the free school he had founded and there it was stripped of all clothing and exposed. This dishonoring of both the death and the corpse was meant to intimidate his relatives and, indeed, everyone in the village. The ritual of exposing Grandfather's corpse went on for several days until even Comrade Song grew bored of it, and then he ordered the daughter-in-law of Uncle Yongjie to toss my grandfather into a sinkhole near the village.

☙

Sinkholes in limestone formations are a peculiar feature of the southern landscape. A deep pit marks an abrupt subsidence in the earth, as if a meteorite had punched a bottomless hole there. As soon as Grandfather's body had been discarded, the persecutions of Eldest Uncle and Second Uncle got underway. The disaster that had come to the plateau was like a bottomless pit.

Eldest Uncle's charge was easy to write: he had been a puppet constable for the old regime. Second Uncle, when you got right down to it, had been just an ordinary person whose crime had been to receive three acres in the division of his father's property. Much of this ground had been cleared and developed for the very first time by them, personally, but the basic policy of the new regime was to exterminate the propertied class, and the imperial directives permitted extreme measures to this end. Moreover, power had been delegated to the point that those executing the policy on the ground enjoyed considerable latitude, which is to say that the head of a work team was empowered to decide whether a person should live or die. There was as yet no legal code at the national level, and of course there were no courts. My father's elder brothers were both arrested. They were young and hadn't heard much about the new order of things, so they tried to reason with their captors. The most effective response to such reasoning was, of course, violence. They were taken under guard to Badong Town. The eldest brother then died under doubtful circumstances and was tossed into the Yangtze; his remains were never found. Second Uncle was sentenced to the notorious labor camp at Shayang.[49] When he was finally released twenty-nine years later and allowed to return home, he had grown old and could no longer remember what crime he had been charged with.

❧

The story isn't over yet. After sustaining this series of blows, my two aunts lost their nerve to go on living. A farming family without a man is in a bad way, and they knew all too well what kind of indignities and outrages awaited them. They each had four children, of which the oldest was only fifteen, and they couldn't bear to face this brood of vulnerable minors. Late at night after my two uncles had been taken away, these two sisters-in-law chose a most pitiable death. They hanged themselves with the same rope, and from the same rafter. Perhaps they thought this shocking end would touch the conscience of their persecutors and the children would be spared.

Second Uncle's daughter was fifteen and now had seven younger children to look after. In the space of one night, the family had lost its entire older generation and I cannot imagine how they endured. When I went back this year and asked her about it, she began weeping the tears of an old woman and could not stop.

The hunt continued for the weapons my family had allegedly stashed away. They even arrested this cousin of mine who was a little older than the rest and made her lead some militiamen to an aunt's house in Guandian Town over in Jianshi County so that it, too, could be ransacked. That aunt, by the way, now well into her eighties, is the only member of my family's older generation who is still alive today. On that trip this year, I sought her out, and she told me it was fortunate that the person to whom she was married at that time was a peasant. It was only when she saw her niece, clad in rags and brought to her door by gun-toting guards, and heard the child sob out her story, that she learned of the calamity which had befallen her family. She upbraided the men, had her village work team attest that her family had concealed no weapons, and declared that whoever had accused her was probably the one who was hiding guns. It was not in her power to assist her nephews and nieces, for her own family was dirt-poor; all she could offer was a bag of cornmeal for the girl to take back with her. Years of hardship followed: of my eight cousins, two starved to death. The four girls married as soon as they could, seeking sustenance like the child-brides of a bygone era who were raised in their husbands' households. The two surviving boys, burdened with bad family backgrounds, were targeted for discrimination and punishment in each of the political campaigns that came along. No one dared marry them. My aunt married her daughter to the elder of the two, and since the couple were so closely related, they did not have children. The younger boy was married in middle age to a widow who had been sterilized, so he didn't have an heir either.

❧

The great campaign of land reform ended in a reign of terror: historical records suggest that more than three million people lost their lives after being classified as landlords. Most of them were hard-working farmers like my grandfather . . . a whole generation of them. When the new regime needed to mobilize the population in its drive for power, these were the people whose skulls served as ensigns of war. Mao's own father had been a landlord: how could he not have known how much of the old man's life had been a struggle? Could he really have thought the meager riches of these people were the fruit of exploitation? It was all a ploy in his struggle for power: did he not say, "Political tactics are the life-blood of the Party"?

When poor peasants and farm laborers and, especially, jobless vagrants obtained the deeds to other people's houses and property, they had to pinch themselves. In the casino of this world, a new god had shuffled the deck and anyone would have thought it a stroke of luck to get something for nothing, so they were delighted to tap-dance into the New Society. But as soon as the regime was established and no longer had to fear a wavering of the peasants' allegiance, a whole set of brilliant programs was unveiled, starting with the mutual-aid groups and proceeding through the coöperatives all the way to the People's Communes.[50] In the tempestuous march forward into Communism, more than thirty million peasants starved along the way. Even today, we are still lamenting the three rural problems,[51] still agitating on behalf of the peasant's fundamental right to be treated like a citizen.

The repercussions of land reform went further. A sharpening of divisions along class lines, and the doctrine of class struggle which was based on it, became from this point onward the most farcical and tragic absurdity of the second half of the twentieth century. In a society founded on an appeal for justice and freedom, people were divided into various grades and ranks, and the highest authorities purposely created opposing camps and fomented hatred to open a chasm between each man and his neighbor, setting them against each other. Of the traditional virtues—humaneness, righteousness, decorum, and trust—nothing remained. The irreducible principles of ethics were gone. Everyone joined to exalt the Wicked, the False, and the Ugly, taking poverty for excellence, and the entire society seethed in an atmosphere of rapine and violence.

The gentry class which for thousands of years had safeguarded a social order based on laws and rites was now demonized, with every imaginable calumny heaped upon their heads. Even when one escaped death, he and his children were sure to suffer decades of discrimination. This was devastating to civil society and its fatal consequences are still with us. Many lost all sense of respect, and misconduct of all kinds spread like a plague. An ancient people sustained internal injuries for which there was no precedent.

๛

Where was my father, then at the height of his youthful vigor, when this disaster struck? Could he have saved his family? Couldn't he have tried? For years I have wondered. After all, Chinese civilization traditionally attaches the greatest importance to one's duty as a son or brother, to the obligations of kinship. How could he have continued blithely on, indifferent to his family's extermination?

At this same time, a popular revolt against land reform finally exploded in three townships of Lichuan County (Wendou, Shaxi, and Changshun — and so it is known to history as the "Wen-Sha-Chang Rebellion"). The main instigator was a man named Fei Wenxue, the son of a small landholder in Shaxi. He was attending college in Wuhan, and when he heard that his father had been executed along with other innocent people, he hurried home. His hometown was as remote and isolated as my father's. But this young man with a high IQ chose the path of vengeance. He made contact with the families of landlords—and many peasants—in the other two counties and launched an uprising in which he put to death more than ten people on the land-reform work team in Wendou. The only one who escaped did so by hiding among the yams piled in a cellar.

Zheng Yonghuai, the author's father, *circa* 1950

Using violence against violence only makes the violence greater. It was just then that my father was appointed Party Secretary in Wendou. The regular army troops under his command, ordered to suppress these bandits, carried out a still greater slaughter. One of my father's comrades-in-arms who is still alive today recalls, "We may have missed a few individuals, but we didn't miss any households"—in other words, in practically every family, young men were interrogated under torture. Who will not crack under duress? There was no end to the names thus obtained of those who were said to be in cahoots with the bandits, and one by one they were all executed.

Fei Wenxue escaped into the ancient forest with a band of followers and my father's small detachment pursued them in a slow and winding chase. There ensued a mortal contest between two sons of landlords, deep in the wooded mountains, and repeatedly one nearly fell into the other's hands. (That will be another story.) Finally, my father invited his adversary to surrender (the District Committee had authorized him to do so) and after a few difficulties had been worked out, Fei Wenxue brought in his troops to surrender their weapons. It had been agreed that the matter would be allowed to drop and he would be treated as an enlightened country gentleman.[52] My father seems to have believed that this was indeed the Party's policy and at that time he became friendly, even brotherly, with Fei. A few months later, a secret order came from the Prefectural government: the Fei clan was to be taken to the city under guard and without publicity. My father was ashamed. He knew he would have to break his word, because the Party had no use for such things as keeping one's word. Fei Wenxue was quickly and secretly put to death, and his loyal followers did not survive the campaign which came soon after to Eliminate Counterrevolutionaries. Thus was one man's rebellion suppressed. His blood trickled into the ground and was lost in the mire; even his story would ravel out in the winds of time.

After he witnessed these acts of cruelty, even supposing my father was aware of the tragedy unfolding more than a hundred miles away in his hometown, what could he have done? That which is called "the organization" has no feeling for the sufferings of individuals. To expect an individual to show courage in the face of overwhelming power is asking too much of human nature. I only came to understand my father's cowardice, his decision to play it safe, after I read an essay recommended by a friend this year.

৩

It was an article about Niu Yinguan—you can look it up online. He came from Xing County in Shanxi and became a member of the underground Party while at Tsinghua University (Yao Yilin, a bit younger than he, was there at the same time). After December 9,[53] the Party dispatched him to Shanxi to join the Standing Committee of the Alliance for National Salvation.[54] He also served as the deputy director of the Party's administrative office in northwestern Shanxi. His father was Niu Youlan, a landlord and industrialist considered an enlightened gentleman and well-known in that part of the country. He is mentioned together with Li Dingming and Liu Shaobai in Mao's *Selected Works*.[55] He not only encouraged his numerous progeny to join the CCP; he himself purchased the equipment for a regiment of the Eighth Route Army, for whom his house at one time served as headquarters. In Xing County, he established an agricultural bank and a munitions factory for the CCP.

Father and son, the two Nius had been benefactors in many ways in that district that was always called one of the liberated areas.[56] But in 1947, when Mao was grappling with Chiang Kai-shek in the contest for power, Mao realized that to get the better of Chiang he needed the peasants more actively on his side. That is when land reform got underway in the areas under CCP control. Here the task was entrusted to Li Jingquan (later Party Secretary in Sichuan during the Cultural Revolution), and Li sought out Niu Youlan for a number of discussions in which he urged him to repudiate his father. Then a large meeting was held for the purpose of "struggling against" Niu. The father knelt at the foot of a stage on which his son was standing. The Peasants' Assembly, which for the most part comprised the loafers and riffraff of the village, pierced his father's nose with an iron wire and ordered him to lead the old man like an ox on parade.[57] Niu Yinguan had no choice: he had to do it. His father wrenched his head away in rage and a bone in his nose was pulled out. The peasants gathered round couldn't bear to watch any more and attacked the work team from all sides and untied the father's bonds. This gentleman, who had given so much to the Communist Party and his community and had served as a representative in the legislature of the border area, went home and refused to eat. Three days later he was dead.

Even though Niu Yinguan had shown such self-control, he was removed from office and sent to the Party School for re-training. The common people throughout this liberated zone were quick to judge him when they heard the harrowing tale: he must be grossly unfilial. Though later he would serve as deputy governor, ranking at the ministerial level, and though he would run the aircraft factory which would produce the Communist regime's first-generation fighter plane, he was nonetheless despised by many of his colleagues. People found it hard to trust a man who could take part in the persecution of his father. This was the cross he bore for the rest of his life. And like my father, he never spoke about his father. No one could know the depth of bitterness in his heart, much less imagine the choice he had made when he had no other choice. Only with the posthumous publication of Yao Yilin's *Hundred-Night Talk*[58] did we learn the facts. The chapter "The Actual Facts of the Historical Record in Shanxi" recounts that during land reform, the eight districts of Xing County saw 1050 people murdered while 863 committed suicide, and a further 63 perished of cold and hunger after being driven out of their homes. Their names are unknown today; in all likelihood many were not landlords but rather peasants who evinced some sympathy for the landlords. I forgave my father, truly, after reading this. Under the pressure of tyranny the social conscience of a people was destroyed, almost without a trace, and we can now understand why during the subsequent campaigns so many denounced or informed on members of their own family and participated in the violence against them. And if we want to regain the bedrock of human nature, we still have a long way to go.

❧

Sociologically, human life is marked by inequality from the start. Only at the most primitive stage of society is it possible for no one to begin with any advantages. After that, differences in family background assure each individual a different starting point. Social Darwinism rests on the survival of the fittest. This is harsh. By ensuring inequitably different starting points for different individuals, it causes a polarization in which the poor are doomed to remain poor forever while the rich own an ever-increasing share of society's resources. Absent a benign government to effect some redistribution, this kind of society must evolve toward an extreme state which makes revolution inevitable. Revolution is a way—the bloodiest way—to shuffle the deck and deal a fresh hand; but since the majority of people are not content to stay at the equal starting-point, competition then begins anew.

Peasant revolts come naturally to China. A few thousand years of history show that we live in a social seismic zone. The rallying-cry of every rebellion has been to divide up the land to equalize rich and poor, but once the power of the State has been wrested away, the fruits of victory are reserved for a minority. What the leaders of each revolution have won is, essentially, the imperial robe: they have never brought forth a new, progressive system to replace the ills of the previous regime. Revolution is an act of violence, in the brilliant formulation of our Great Leader. And violence is inevitably irrational and must bring a paroxysm of ruin. Chinese civilization has gone through this strange cycle again and again, and appears unable to advance beyond it.

If there were no revolution, then by implication the whole of society would have gone on acquiescing in injustice and tyranny. Although a maxim goes as far back as Mencius to the effect that the people should count for more than the sovereign,[59] after three thousand years we have yet to attain a true republic. The declaration of Sun Wukong, "Emperors take turns on the throne: next year it's my family's turn," never implied peaceful discussion and an election but was always about fighting for power.[60] Hong Xiuquan conquered half the country and promoted his Heavenly Dynasty's system for dividing and managing the land, ostensibly to give people equal chances.[61] But when you learn more about his Heavenly Kingdom, you realize it was an utter disaster for the nation.

Under the banner of "national revolution," Sun Yat-Sen made his move through the Wuchang Uprising and finally united forces from the North and the South, forcing the Qing Emperor's abdication. This revolution was not at its heart a peasants' insurrection for land rights; therefore, under the Republic, society carried on largely as before, with the Qing system of land ownership intact. Sun was by no means unaware that three hundred years after the Manchu redistribution there had once more arisen an extreme inequality between rich and poor. Though he raised the cry, "The land to him that tills it!," he was sufficiently familiar with Western civilization to know that plundering people was unjust, no matter what rationalizations it might be clothed in. During the reign of Chiang Kai-shek, the government had the idea of evening out land ownership by purchasing tracts, but it didn't have enough money.

It's obvious today that by the 1940s the land issue was a real problem. When the majority sank into poverty because they owned no (or little) land, the situation became genuinely dangerous. It was now a problem which professional revolutionaries could turn to their advantage.

❧

Originally Communism was no more than an economic doctrine, and at best a blueprint for Utopia born out of a foolish political fantasy. But thanks to Lenin it evolved into a totalitarian system of government founded on national revolution, and in this form the Third International spread it to other poor countries where it had a weighty and tragic impact on history: hundreds of millions of lives were shoveled into the ditches of the twentieth century. Marx and Engels, the doctrine's parents, did not foresee this. Indeed, when Engels addressed the land question, the solution he recommended was for the government to buy up land and distribute it to the poor.[62] This was the humanitarian appeal of Marxism and it's why, in the beginning, it attracted many intellectuals who had a social conscience.

If we can see past the myth-making and obfuscations of history, it is clear that most of the representatives who attended the First Party Congress[63] were well-meaning and well-educated people. They were youths with a sense of justice, indignant at the status quo, and they sought a better ordering of society. That is why when this somewhat aca-

63

demic association degenerated into a criminal gang, most of that first batch of representatives chose to resign.[64] In those days, the KMT was not in power, either. For the sake of the Northern Expedition, Sun Yat-sen proposed to ally with Russia and the Communists and to give support to farmers and workers. This led to the collaboration of the two parties, and the CCP seized the chance to expand its power-base at the grassroots. While the KMT set up its base at Wuhan, the countryside in several southern provinces was under the control of the CCP and they launched a large-scale peasant movement. Landlords and the gentry class were plundered. At the time, the portfolio for peasant and worker affairs was in Mao's hands. Reading his *Report on the Peasant Movement in Hunan*, with its implicit endorsement of violent means, one can discern the starting point and pattern of later land reform.

The society of the time reacted to this violent anarchy with shock and condemnation. After all, lynching and pillaging hardly accorded with the ideal of the Three Principles of the People.[65] Society needed to be reformed; the gulf between rich and poor needed to be evened out; this is what the government had to accomplish, but gradually and by well-organized means. If the mob runs riot and no justice can be secured, and in fact the red tide unleashes social upheaval across large swaths of territory—that's something not even today's so-called People's Democratic Dictatorship would tolerate. So when Chiang Kai-shek took over Shanghai he decided to wipe out the CCP and suppress the disorders. Innumerable young idealists became sacrificial victims. In one night known to history as the May 21 Incident, the two parties became implacable foes.[66] Immediately afterward, Mao Zedong and Zhou Enlai launched an armed uprising[67] and went from being local strongmen to setting up a rival regime that ruled part of the country. The rivalry between the parties thus grew into a clash between governments that would ultimately struggle for control of the entire nation. Our country entered a long period of darkness and bloodshed. Today we call this chapter of history the first revolutionary war over the land. The land . . . oh, the land! It seems that many lives must be buried there for it to bring forth flowers and grain.

Tsarist Russia practiced a village commune system in which land was redistributed at fixed intervals.[68] There were rich peasants, but there were no landlords, and only 5% of the land was in the hands of independent farmers. The Bolsheviks were an urban faction who never had much sympathy for the peasantry. After the October Revolution the Soviet government had to expend a great deal of energy fighting the peasants in order to collect grain taxes. For a lasting solution to this problem, in 1921 Stalin began the forced collectivization of the farming villages and found it necessary to dispatch the regular army into the countryside, where it battled the armed peasantry. After the pointless slaughter of too many people, the process was finally brought to an end in 1937. One of its effects was that the peasants ate most of their livestock, and agriculture regressed to the point of food shortages. So when the Chinese Communist Party announced plans for land reform in 1946, the usually rash and reckless Stalin advised Mao to be very, very careful about that.

But Mao could not win the Civil War without the support that land reform would bring him. His early experiences in Hunan had convinced him that he could not overcome the government's armed forces unless he completely overthrew the existing social order. Chiang Kai-shek finally understood the principles at stake after his defeated army went to Taiwan: unless he solved the problem of the countryside, he would always be sitting on top of a volcano. That is why the KMT undertook land reform on Taiwan in the 1950s[69]—but they went about it a little differently and followed Engels's prescription of buying out the landowners. The state put up the capital for the purchase and transferred ownership to the farmers. The landlords took their funds to the cities, where they started developing industry and commerce. No need to comment on how the two approaches worked out on opposite sides of the Strait.

☙

The dreadful fate of the landlords and rich peasants did not cease with the completion of land reform. That was but the beginning of an unending persecution. In all the political campaigns that followed, elements of the landlord and rich-peasant class, together with their children, were forever pilloried and there was no end to their humiliations. When the Cultural Revolution came, discrimination and abuse reached bizarre heights.

The thought often occurs to me that my childhood ended at age four.[70] One summer afternoon I caught sight of a crowd of men and women, with machetes and rifles on their shoulders, coming down one of the streets of our small town. My father was in front of them. He was wearing a tall hat glued out of paper and his whole face was smeared with grime. I thought this was some kind of comic performance and found his make-up amusing, so I dashed home to announce the fun. My mother and grandmother were sitting there in tears and I realized abruptly that something very grave had befallen our family. In 1968, when my elder sister led me by the hand to register at our village elementary school, along the way she coached me how to respond to the teacher's questions, of which the crucial one would be:

Q. Family class status?
A. Landlord.

I already had an inkling that this was not a title of honor. For the next eight years, at the start of each school year I, like other children born to landlord or rich-peasant families, would time my arrival for an hour when the other students wouldn't be there. We didn't want to be found out and laughed to scorn.

As children, our generation grew used to the fact that many horrors were a part of life. Because she was a landlord's wife, the mother of one of my classmates was strung up and beaten with her hands bound behind her back. One wintry day when the river was bone-chilling, a few old neighbors of ours who had once been landlords were ordered into the water to dredge for a gun cache. Today I know that many worse things were occurring in our country at that time. In Dao County in Hunan, and in the Daxing district of Beijing, there was a brief, tragic period when it was standard procedure to execute the entire families of landlords and rich peasants. How could hatred be nurtured to the point of such utter ruthlessness?

In order to stir up the peasantry during the 1940s, a hack writer invented the character of Huang Shiren. The '50s saw the creation of Nan Batian and Skin-flayer Zhou.[71] During the Cultural Revolution, wanting a real-life figure resembling these three despots, Sichuan trotted out Liu Wencai. The stories of his dungeon with waist-high water and the rent-collection courtyard had an enormous influence. Every region unearthed its own record of appallingly heinous landlords, enabling class struggle to remain the focus of discussion day after day, month after month, year after year.[72] In our time a friend of mine, after much research, has written *The Truth about Liu Wencai*. He found that every part of the legend was either exaggerated or completely fabricated.[73] The publication of this work must have touched a nerve, for its distribution was immediately forbidden.

I grew up in the border town of Lichuan. It, too, had an infamous landlord, a man by the name of Li Gaiwu. In that mountainous zone between two provinces, he left behind a manor of majestic beauty called Great Well which now, interestingly enough, has become a nationally-protected cultural site. But during land reform he was broiled alive on a gridiron. In their time in the hill country, what a distinguished family the Li clan were! And now hardly a single one survives to carry on the line. In peasants' homes there I came across fragments of the Li family precepts, rules that breathed decency and integrity. This was the traditional culture that kept order in the countryside, passed on from generation to generation for a few thousand years. We threw it all away, and it won't be easy to get it back.

☙

When I was growing up my father never told us his whole story. His Party membership went way, way back, and he had been a grass-roots cadre; yet he always seemed to be trying terribly hard on account of his family background, as if he sensed the ground could give way beneath his feet at any moment. It was as if he felt he still had a debt to pay to this society on account of his father. He was afraid to contact his family and never in his life went back to the place he'd been born. He hid the wounds in his soul.

In 1978 Second Uncle came to visit us after he was released from prison. It startled me to see for the first time an old man who looked uncannily like my father. It had been thirty years since the brothers saw each other. The meeting lacked the joy that is typical when people meet again after surviving a disaster; there was too much in their hearts, and it was too deep and too heavy. Great sorrow, like great joy, is often at a loss for words. The two old men kept their conversation secret from us; I have no way to know what bitterness may have been expressed between them behind that closed bedroom door, or whether my father was, for once in his life, moved to tears.

Second Uncle went back alone to his native town in the hill country where his children were eking out a living. He had lost his land, of course, and could not call even the humblest house his home: he had to lodge in a cave outside the village, and he found work as a goatherd to sustain him in his guttering decline. Later—a year before my father—he softly crumpled away.

Shortly before his own passing, my father said he was going to take me back to his hometown after I got out. Then when he died, a nephew who had visited him near the end told me my father had harbored the hope that in better days I would make that journey and fill in the sinkhole where Grandfather's body had been thrown. He had asked that I go there to set Grandfather's grave to rights and erect a monument. From this deathbed request I finally glimpsed the bitter grief my father had carried in his heart all those years. His remorse about his father was something the local Party apparatus would never allow him to go and express, and it lingered as a life-long regret.

In September 2005 I went to my ancestral home for the first time and found that dark chasm. Together with my sisters, I fulfilled my father's last wish, for after covering the hole we had an epitaph engraved. The inscription read:[74]

The Zheng family in the land of Enshi was descended from the five primordial clans of the Ba people. Our ancestors took refuge in this district, though the details, and even the era when they came, are uncertain. It was our grandfather the honorable Zhenlüe whose hard work established this house. Modest were his fields and his manor. He founded a free school and arbitrated the people's disputes. As a squire he was a virtuous elder. The twenty-sixth year[75], when the dynasty changed, brought calamity upon the entire family. Yearning for dignity, the honorable

Zhenlüe could not bear disgrace. In April of the twenty-eighth year he hanged himself. (Of our two uncles, one perished in prison and the other was banished. Their wives both hanged themselves. Our father avoided these events, for he had enrolled in college elsewhere.) Neighbors promptly buried the body in the sinkhole. Thereafter war and tumult scattered his kin. For years, a bitter cold. Fortunately the Way of Heaven was not extinct, and the good deeds of our ancestors continued to protect us: the family line flourished anew. Therefore here and now we have moved the mountainous earth and graven a stone to commemorate our grandfather's beneficence and fulfill our father's wish. And so we pray:

> *May the hills surround and protect this resting-place.*
> *May the waters that flow past keep it verdant.*
> *May his noble spirit endure.*
> *May we remember him with reverence forever.*

An Education in Cruelty

Is human cruelty an instinct of our animal nature or a genetic trait? Is it a dysfunction forced on us by a particular kind of society or does it arise from an individual's education and upbringing? Can we adapt Tolstoy's celebrated dictum to say that all good people are basically alike, but every cruel person is cruel in his own way?

Long ago while I was incarcerated, my mother wrote to tell me that my daughter (who at that time was not quite six years old and didn't know her father) had undergone a troubling personality change. She would take a kettleful of boiling water, for example, and slowly pour it into the fish-tank and watch the fish struggle desperately with no way to escape, till at last they were scalded to death. My mother was afraid the child's play revealed a cruel streak. The news shocked me, but I realized on some level that almost all human cruelty partakes of the nature of a game, and in a great many games there is an implicit cruelty.

I didn't hold it against my daughter. One could attribute her behavior to immaturity, the lack of a father-figure, and the fact she had not yet received any precepts about the safe-guarding of life—precepts more or less religious in origin, but typical of civilized society. She was still in a state of primitive barbarism that recapitulated the early history of the human race. But then I thought back to the rough childhood I had endured in a remote small town, and it dawned on me that by growing up in this country I had received a whole education in cruelty. Considering that adults still play (or at least tolerate) all kinds of sick, cruel games, I'd be ashamed to judge a child harshly.

That famous period of ten years commenced when I was four years old[76] and found me in the state of nature. There was at that time no regular kindergarten or preschool instruction, and naturally there was a complete lack of educational pastimes. The first game I learned from the older boys in the village was to catch a toad out in the fields and make a little kiln of mud, inside which we'd spread a layer of quicklime. We'd put the toad inside and seal up the kiln with thin streaks of clay, leaving a little hole on top through which to pour cold water. On contact with water, the quicklime was energized and generated a great deal of heat, and as the steam curled up, there rang out a croaking cry of tortured pain, first very strong and then fading away. When the steam and the noise were both finished, we'd rake open the mud kiln to find that the toad's ugly skin had peeled off, exposing the trunk of its body, translucent and glowing like the flesh of a newborn child; for in death the toad revealed a beauty of extreme purity.

Who had invented so cruel a pastime? The children must have come to it by imitation, but what exactly were they imitating?

☙

For years I have had a recurring dream in which I am standing naked under the blue sky of late autumn, trying to soak up enough sunlight to survive the winter—for the winter is going to be exceptionally cold. The rays of the setting sun slant over the high wall behind me, casting an enlarged shadow of me on the wall in front. The shadow of the electrified wires just happens to cross at my neck, making the silhouette of my head look like a wild fruit overripe amid a tangle of withered vines.

This made me realize that if immersed in a savage reality, the heart becomes inured to cruelty: it has to. This scene, which I had actually experienced, was so frightening at the time that it was later fashioned into the image of a recurring dream during a long spell of ordinary life. I would like to identify the moment when I began taking cruelty as a matter of course. When did we start to accept malice and violence as a part of normal life, excusable and unchecked by any law?

I was six . . . yes, I was six years old and in the first grade. Early autumn, 1968. When school let out, the students were assembled and a vigorous teacher took apart a big broom and gave each of us children one of the bamboo stems. Then we lined up and headed off to administer a beating to a thief. When our troop of scouts came marching down the street, the townsfolk who had surrounded the thief raised a jolly cheer. The thief had been made to stand on a cement culvert pipe. His shirt was tattered and his trouser-legs had been rolled up over his knees as if he had just come in from the paddies, and he was shod in straw sandals. These particulars are etched in my memory because our height reached just about to the man's ankles. The grown-ups were loudly urging us on, "Beat him! Beat him!" and thus the small town's Carnival of the Thief got underway.

We schoolchildren from the village ranged in age from six to sixteen and, giddy at being for the first time encouraged by adults to beat up another adult, we didn't hold back. Lashed like a top by countless bamboo rods, that middle-aged thief began to hop and prance along the pipe in a dance that never let up. There was no escape. To whichever side he was driven, a dense screaming throng was waiting to whip him. I distinctly remember the coarse skin of his calves, still a little muddy, slowly turning from red to purple, then gradually swelling and turning white and translucent like a turnip. He kept uttering little cries and desperately flailing his hands and feet. The drops of his sweat fell like rain and there shone from his eyes the cold light of death. I swung at him a few times. Then, frightened, I held back, but the grown-ups and the other children were still engrossed in the delightful sport they had devised. Finally I noticed that he had grown so hoarse that his mouth opened and shut soundlessly like a fish and his body was shaking like a kite off-kilter, and when one more blow came, the blow that was one too many, he fell with a crash . . .

When first summoned round him, we had learned from the grown-ups' execrations that he had been arrested for trying to pilfer three feet of cloth from a tailor's shop. He was a peasant come in from the country to attend the fair. Remorse haunted me later. I kept thinking that life had prepared the same winter for us both; in fact his kids, about my age, wore rags and he had no money to make them warmer. And on this day he had spied those fatal three feet of cloth. Each time I recall the scene, the pain reaches a bit deeper. Having written thus far, I find tears running down my face and I realize that this was the beginning of my education in cruelty.

❧

It's often hard to identify the moral quality that makes some hurtful acts cruel. If in a room full of mosquitoes we were to shut the doors and windows and light a coil of insecticide in order to exterminate the pests, no one would condemn us. What about mice? Well, they spread disease and steal food, so they too deserve to be exterminated. As for the means employed to exterminate them, people don't usually inquire too closely.

When I was about ten, my mother sent me to the coal mine because my father was being punished in all sorts of ways after being "knocked down." It had proven too much for one of his colleagues who had already committed suicide. Mother was worried and sent me to keep him company, thus introducing me to the real life of the working class. There were many rats in the mine then, and the men who constantly risked death in the pit had nothing in the way of entertainment, so in their moments of free time they tried exterminating the rats for fun. They used all their wiles to capture a rat alive. Then they'd stuff raw soybeans into its rectum and sew up the anus. The soybeans would expand inside the rat's body and drive it mad with pain; then they'd let it go and watch it run around in a frenzy, careening back to its home where it bit and scratched at its own kind, creating a rousing spectacle of mutual annihilation: this trick was more devastating than any poison. Or they would tie a wad of cotton soaked in gasoline to a rat's tail and release it after setting the cotton aflame, and then watch with pleasure as the little fireball ran around crazily. These scenes frightened me. Nothing but disgust and hatred made them torture rats so: was this the human race's idea of justice?

And what of how humans massacre each other? The Nazis' hatred for the Jews, and the genocide they perpetrated, are too well-known to need recounting here. The hatred we once harbored for what was called the exploiting class seems practically on the same level. In my part of the country there was major landholder named Li Gaiwu; in the era of land reform he was crammed into a cage by angry peasants who then propped him over a fire and roasted him alive. Such a drawn-out, hideous death: none of us has even an inkling of the pain. If we review our penal history with its "death by a thousand cuts" and violent forms of sterilization and other such punishments, it is hard to believe we are a people under the guidance of reason.

❧

A lesson taught us from our earliest years was that "Kindness to the enemy is cruelty to the People," and this political ethic has always guided our social life. A maxim which Party members consider the Golden Rule demands that we treat comrades with the warmth of springtime, but to the enemy we must be like the autumn wind that blows away dead leaves without mercy. We recognize empathy as a basic element of human nature; the Buddha said that only with compassion can living creatures exist. To be without empathy, to be ruthless, means we need only take a political stand and can dispense with fundamental human considerations and instinctive sympathies. When dealing with outsiders (i.e., enemies), we may go to any length and take any measures to punish them.

In the natural order, it's hard to distinguish between noxious insects and those that do some good. How accurately then are we likely to differentiate between enemies and friends, when all are of our own kind? The final decision will inevitably be based on power. When the highest authorities declared that sparrows were pests, these innocent creatures had to be exterminated by the entire people acting in concert. For these little birds, the sky suddenly shrank; they were massacred; they fell in droves, dead from exhaustion as they struggled to flee the country. If birds fare thus, how can men endure? When we calmly look back on the whole twentieth century and consider all the people we called enemies and the animals we called pests, how many of them look entirely evil or destructive from today's vantage point? Those poor teachers, or fellow-soldiers, or relatives or neighbors might, depending on the unfathomably mutable dispositions of the supreme authorities, flourish at morn to be cut down at night. Is there anyone who has not tasted this cruelty?

In 1976 I was a student in early middle school in my small town. That year there was a great deal of grief and laughter in our country, emotions that took many forms and were seldom openly expressed.[77] Historians will see this as a year of transition. That winter, we students were taken as a group to participate in a public trial and sentencing at which a counterrevolutionary named Yang Wensheng was to be shot.

From what we could make out of the not-very-clear verdict, this was a man so bad that even his death would scarcely suffice to appease the People's wrath. His crime was that when high authorities had arrested the Gang of Four, he insisted that—based on the principles and examples of historical fiction—this had been a palace coup. He was constantly making speeches and pasting up large-character posters opposing the Central Government under Hua Guofeng. He called on people to guard the heritage of Mao while resolutely opposing the return of the capitalist-roader.[78] Prior to this, he had been well-known in town as part of the extremist faction of the Red Guard and had, to be sure, persecuted some of the local cadres.

In those days, many of the ancient formalities were still observed while a prisoner awaited execution. The man was tightly bound with ropes and once the sentence had been read aloud, they thrust down the back of his shirt a sharp stick on which the name of his crime had been written. I saw him grimace with pain then, but he was bound so tight he couldn't cry out. A few of us bold kids hopped on our bicycles and followed the prison van to the undeveloped land outside the town. There he was lifted down out of the van and kicked to his knees on the frozen ground. From less than a meter away, the executioner deftly fired at the man's back and he pitched forward. Though his crumpled body shuddered a few times, he soon became still as the echo of the shot reverberated off the surrounding hills. A throng of all ages, male and female, had gathered to watch. In a society rife with tedium, an execution served much the same function as a wedding banquet: the man's death provided a little zest for the masses. A grown-up went and turned over the body and loosened the clothes, and we were startled to see blood still flowing from the bullet-hole on the left side of his chest, as the last of his body's warmth dispersed upon the wintry earth.

Thus was a life disposed of. Some time before, in the north a woman named Zhang Zhixin had been put to death in an even more brutal fashion.[79] These two people were charged with the same crime, though in substance their actions were diametrically opposite. We could say that Zhang died for her wisdom and clear vision, while Yang died for his folly and stubbornness. What got both of them in trouble was that at that stage of history each was a person who stuck to his convictions and expressed them; how the world later gauged the validity of their beliefs is irrelevant. They were punished as criminals for nothing but their expressed opinions: they led no rebellion, committed no murders, burned no buildings. Every civilized country writes freedom of speech into its constitution as the citizens' right. Yet for attempting to exercise this simple right, Zhang became a tragic hero and Yang remains forever a fool.

As we wander through this world, the fleeting pleasures of the senses make us cling to life, and the religious ideal of self-sacrifice presupposes heroic virtue. To survive, we must vie with other species for the means of life and if an instinctive animosity arises from this situation, it is hard to fault men for it. But when there is a life-and-death struggle of one man against another, or of tribe against tribe and nation against nation, and we must plot against one another and fight at close quarters: what moral criteria are laid down for human nature then? Can't some principle always be found, such as individualism, nationalism, or patriotism, that will let us bend the rules and justify our violence?

When I ask these questions about the history of individuals, or the background of my relatives and friends, or the stories (both factual and imagined) of our people, I usually am left unsure what moral standards should be applied. The common people worship Heaven and Earth, and this teaches them reverence. The gentleman stays far from the kitchen and thus cultivates compunction.[80] Reverence leads to awe, and compunction leads to love. Now if everyone were imbued with awe and love, perhaps there would be no need for religion, and we could still manage to live saintly lives. The difficulty comes when you dwell in an atheistic country where constant propaganda has exalted scientific fundamentalism into an overarching value, and where revolution and violent rebellion (such as led by Li Zicheng and Hong Xiuquan[81]) are the stuff of heroic legends. Is it possible to feel any awe under these circumstances? Can all the laws in the world check the malice latent in our nature, especially since it has been repeatedly encouraged and sanctioned?

In the perilous year 1949 my father, the son of a small landholder, sought safety by joining the new government. Calamities befell his family during land reform, but he became a hero—in another county—in the fight to suppress the 'bandits.' My father always tried to avoid discussing his past, rather as a bitter old man who had failed in life would fear encountering a woman he had loved in his youth, but I was able to piece together his story from the recollections of some who had known him back then. In that cruel time, he had to be particularly ruthless, since otherwise his loyalty would have been doubted on account of his background. When I think how he trapped and killed those fierce brave men of the highlands and signed death-warrants for land-lords who had worked hard (like his own father) for every-thing they had, I am sure that this was not how he wanted to act. He was not stupid. He couldn't have thought he was being fair, but he knew that if he revealed even a hint of human kindness, it would give others a reason to mark him for liquidation. It was like the organized-crime families in which junior mobsters must commit a murder as soon as they are recruited, to give proof of their staunchness. He had no choice.

After the Uprising of the Three Townships had been quelled,[82] his pacification squad took about a dozen prison-ers. From the county seat came orders to bring them into town, but my father had only two armed men with him. With their hands tied behind their backs, the bandits were marched toward the city, but they dragged their feet enough that nightfall found all of them still in a desolate part of the country. It was a dangerous situation. My father's two subor-dinates suggested killing the prisoners and reporting they'd been shot while trying to escape. He was in charge; it was his call. For his men's safety, he consented. The prisoners' bonds were untied and they were told to run for it and take their chances. The three militiamen opened fire on the scattering fugitives in the moonlight, and hardly any managed to get away alive.

This was the cruelty that the revolution required. Long before, our Leader had used a series of parallel sentences to explain for us exactly what is meant by revolution: "an act of violence."[83] In our childhood, this startling passage was popularized as a song whose terrifying refrain echoed through the land. To its melody, kids gracefully brandished belts (and whipped their classmates who came from bad class backgrounds), forced their teachers to eat excrement, raided homes and pillaged them, and hounded innumerable innocents to death. I reckon that few in my generation were squeamish at the sight of blood, because we had seen so much of it. We had grown accustomed to all life's cruelty and nothing shocked us anymore.

❧

Apart from cases in which people are forced to be cruel, I am often puzzled whether cruelty stems from ignorance or hatred. Or could there be other causes than these two? After reading the letter from my mother, I remembered something that happened when my daughter was even younger and we lived together for intervals. She was a little more than one year old, still quite skittish in the presence of unfamiliar faces. Though her father, I was much like a transient visitor, and her tantrums left me at a loss. The best I could think to do was to carry her in my arms to the fishtank. It worked: the swaying, glittering fish caught her attention and she stopped crying. At first her tearful eyes tracked the soundless dance of the fish, and then when the fish tired and stopped moving, she reached out her little hand to slap the glass and stir them up. Startled, they broke in all directions and bumped into the glass as they fled. Only after some time did peace return. Then she'd bang the glass again, and once more the fish would flit around wildly. Eventually my daughter smiled through her tears. Perhaps she realized her power to tease these magical little elfin creatures and was pleased with herself.

When the game staled through repetition, she required more stimulation and ordered me to hold her closer to the tank. Then, to my surprise, she reached into the water to grab at the flustered fish. She was brazen about it and seemed perfectly confident that these small weak animals could do her no harm. What if they had been scorpions? What makes a child know instinctively whether it is safe or dangerous to tease a particular kind of animal? Do we have an innate ability to infer from the aesthetics of a creature's form whether it is innocuous? The fish could not long evade her grasp, and when she'd got one, its panicked wriggling startled her and she threw it on the floor, where it flopped about like a mechanical toy before lying still. She burst into laughter.

Thus I realized that like me, my daughter was fond of fish. But her love expressed itself by tormenting the object of her love. This amorous baiting, as well as the full-blown cruelty to which it can lead, is often seen between grown-up lovers. Milan Kundera says in one of his novels, "They loved each other, but each put the other through Hell."[84] Cruelty that arises from attraction or love may be hard to understand, but it is all around us. My provisional term for it is 'affectionate cruelty.'

❧

From its origin to its dying-out in the life of our society, the term "rectification of styles" has a history spanning no more than half a century.[85] Yet this term—not, on the face of it, a harsh one—laid waste the spirit of our people and to this day one can discern the scars it left behind.

For my generation the fear wrought by this term, a terror from which there was no escape, started in elementary school. At that time I had no inkling where the term came from; I didn't know it had been invented at Yan'an and could make our parents' generation blanch with fear. But when the term came back and repeatedly invaded our childhood, it inspired a dread which lingers with me to this day.

I don't know how those who crafted this country's educational system could have wanted to introduce the cruel ways of adult factional strife into the lives of inexperienced children. But I know that each semester, I quailed in anticipation of the Rectification campaign. Directed at children, it employed the same kinds of threats and blandishments as the adult version and taught a host of naturally kind and honest children how to denounce each other secretly. Although the substance of those accusations now sounds absurd—indeed, ridiculous—the seed of malice was being sown in our young hearts. When you saw a trusted friend step forward to denounce you, righteously, for some childish transgression that you had committed with him, you could not help feeling that human affairs and human nature were treacherous. In the train of betrayal and denunciation always came criticism and mockery, as every child lost all sense of decorum in an orgy of backbiting. Children's innate sense of dignity and sincerity crumbled, to be replaced by a grown-up cunning and the skill to make others take the blame. I can still remember a girl from middle school, a lovely and gentle girl with a thick dark braid. Perhaps because her parents came from the provincial capital, she was a bit more mature in mind and feeling than the rest of us. In the course of one campaign for the Rectification of Styles, a classmate who was her closest girlfriend turned on her and reported hearing her say that she loved to look into the limpid eyes of a certain boy and often dreamed about him. The informer announced this in a tone of the strictest propriety, and the whole room rocked with laughter. Stunned, the innocent girl turned very pale, and then her face and ears flushed crimson and she ducked her head under her desk and cried in anguish. She wept in despair like a widow who has been caught in the act of adultery, and it made me and my peers, all equally confused in our teenage crushes, shiver with fear. A scarlet letter of shame was etched into the heart of a thirteen-year-old girl. She could not possibly remain in that school. Her family pulled her out and sent her to live with relatives in Wuhan, and later she was married off at an early age and became a housewife who sold snacks at a counter. After seeing how quickly a beauty and her youthful innocence were trashed, who could still put any trust in childhood friendship?

Informing, denunciation, betrayal, even entrapment: these defined the ethos of my world from childhood on, and there was no defense against them. What kind of a motherland would wish her children, at what ought to be a tender age, to learn such ruthless arts of survival? In today's society

I sense insecurity and constant danger everywhere, and most of it is rooted in the atmosphere of conspiracy and treachery that was fostered in our education.

❧

What clings to all my memories of the time before 1976 is the smell of blood. I remember, when I was about eight, passing through the courtyard of the District Office at Wangying Town as dusk fell. Suddenly I saw some townsmen tie a peasant's hands behind his back and hang him by the arms from a pear tree. The pear trees were then in bloom; the air was filled with their soft scent and the peasant's screams. The rope that bound his arms passed over a branch and another townsman gripped it from below. When the rest of the group roared, "You're not talking yet?" the rope would be pulled, the peasant's feet would rise higher off the ground, and the ripping in his arms would grow more excruciating.

When he had been hoisted all the way up among the flowers, his sweat fell like rain and his face turned as pale as the pear-blossoms. While he writhed and pleaded, he shook the tree and released a gentle fragrance as petals fell to earth. I stared blankly at the tableau; to this day I cannot fathom the cruelty necessary to take a stranger, tie his hands behind his back, and hoist him by them into the air.

When I became a policeman, a veteran officer cheerfully explained to me that this kind of interrogation, in which the hands are tied behind the back and the prisoner is hung by them, usually should not be protracted beyond a half-hour. Any longer than that, and the suspect's arms will be permanently crippled. I found his well-intentioned advice horrifying, and it brought back the memory of the scene I'd witnessed as a child; it occurred to me with a chill that this rule of thumb must have been distilled from many years' worth of experiments.

But had this interrogation technique stopped being used? In a precinct house where I was assisting with a case in 1988, I was forced to witness a comparable scene. The Chief was quite experienced and, making use of heavy iron shackles, had placed the suspect in an awkward position named after a martial arts move. The two hands were shackled together behind the back, one reaching down with the elbow over the head while the other reached up from the waist. In this position the suspect was forced to kneel for a long time and the Chief left me to keep an eye on him. Being new to the profession, I was in no position to interfere and watched helplessly until the suspect passed out. Then I went to call the Chief to come take the heavy cuffs off him. The Chief exchanged the position of the two arms and continued the treatment.

I am by no means of a cruel temperament. How then could I witness a scene like this one and—though I felt some sympathy—act as though nothing was out of the ordinary? Later on, when I myself had become a convict, I thought a lot about this and realized that the training in cruelty which we'd received from our childhood had worn a callus on my soul. This unfeeling callus progressively hobbled our conscience and made us numb to human suffering. What's more, our cowardice overwhelmed the little pity we could still feel, so we lacked the guts as well as the ability to change

The author in his police uniform, 1988

the system to which we'd grown habituated. When I heard the cries of a man being interrogated under torture, I didn't dare put a stop to it, because I submitted to the uniform I wore. The uniform short-circuited my conscience; for a while I ascribed to it a supernatural power. Consequently when one day another man wearing that uniform struck me in the forehead with an electrified baton, there was nothing for me to say. Neither of us felt any personal animosity; it was only that his education led him to treat me as a foe.

The author as a convict at Wuhan, early 1990s

Who, then, was the unseen Founder behind these countless acts of cruelty? Can we blame oppressive officials, those stock figures who have been passed down through the generations in a certain style of biographical history? Or is the toxin of this cruelty contained in the cultural traditions of our people?

ℭℐ

The elementary education which my generation received had hatred as its starting-point. Teachers invented for us an unspeakably evil Old Society, and made everyone sing each day, with grief and indignation, the song:

> *In the Old Society, whips lashed my flesh,*
> *And Mother could but weep.*[86]

And now it was necessary for us to

> *Seize the whip and lash the foe.*

This is how the violence and cruelty of youth were ignited, and the force thus released spread inevitably to the whole of society, polluting the manners and morals of that era down to the present day.

When the superintendent of a Detention and Transfer Center can incite the common people who've been locked up there to maltreat each other so badly that some of them die; when street-level Code Enforcers can wantonly chase down a peddler with their clubs, and go so far as to beat to death a bystander who photographs them; when soldiers can open fire on students and kill them without compunction, without any misgivings at all . . . could all these unconscionable acts of wickedness reflect the impact of education throughout society?

These days, I can find on the Internet a great many angry young men who rage against Japan and are itching to attack Taiwan. *Rape them, kill them, nuke them,* they roar against

91

those who—in their minds—are enemies or traitors to China. It makes me very sad. These kids were untouched by the Cultural Revolution. They don't even know about 1989. They didn't receive the barbaric education we did. Whence came these cruel attitudes? If an evil administration were to take power, arising from and supported by people such as these youths, who knows what hideous crimes this country would inflict upon the world?

Clearly, some system that inculcates cruelty is still at work in our society; it has always been at work, spreading its influence unseen. The tension between oppressive officials and violent mobs grows ever worse, and the worst in human nature is brought to flower. For it is easy to cultivate hatred and cruelty among men; to propagate love, alas, is hard. When I consider the dreadful possibilities, I have a feeling that the peace of this night will prove fragile and short-lived. I can only guess what lies out there in the dark, but this vast city cocooned in insatiable self-indulgence makes me shudder with fear.

Brother Blind Man

When I returned to the small town of Wangying on official business in 1985, the flagstones of the lanes had been paved over with asphalt and the stilt houses along the river had been replaced by brownstones with tile roofs, and even the winding river itself had been straightened into a canal where, though the water still flowed, neither sandy banks nor eddying pools nor darting schools of fish were any longer to be seen.

What had been a way-station for horse-drawn coaches was now the waiting room for a bus terminal, and bustling peddlers hawked all kinds of home-made pastry in the street. Coming back after ten years I found myself surrounded by unfamiliar faces and stood there at a loss, unsure with which family I might lodge. In this moment of perplexity I heard the clack of castanets.[87] Turning toward the sound I saw none other than Brother Blind Man leaning on a weathered bamboo walking-stick. He stood relaxed at the end of the bridge, swinging the two clappers in an easy-going rhythm. He sang no song and uttered no plea, apparently unconcerned about receiving any money for his performance. His stillness suggested a transcendent disdain for the clamorous world around him. He had the demeanor of a sage of ancient

93

times who had been waiting there for years to direct some gentleman who had truly lost his way.

With a shout of "Brother Blind Man!" I ran to him. He gripped my hand and said quickly, "Don't make a sound. Let's see if I can tell who you are." It had been ten years; I had grown from a boy into a man, and of course my voice had changed. He ran his fingers gently over my hand and cocked his head in concentration. Softly he murmured, "Don't tell me, don't tell me," in the same tone with which one would comfort a frightened child. I noticed he still wore a patchwork of oft-mended clothes, with straw sandals on his feet, and in the sunlight his swarthy skin gleamed like black lacquerware. He had aged visibly, and the snowy white that flecked his hair and beard brought to mind the stubble of a rice paddy on a winter morning or under moonlight. His eyes blinked rapidly and they still had the gleam of an old well that has frozen over. Was it possible for his coarse fingers, which had carefully felt tens of thousands of hands, to recognize the bone structure of a boy from long ago? Suddenly he exclaimed, "Oh! Is it you, Little Furball?"[88] He grinned with a joy that seemed to take possession of his whole frame. Even more moved, I cried, "Brother Blind Man, you still remember me?"

He was old enough for me to have addressed him as "Uncle," but the whole town without distinction of age had always called him Brother Blind Man, so we kids had called him that too. He had been a "picked-up kid."[89] No one knew who his father had been, and when his mother brought the child with her upon marrying into a Wang family, he had taken the surname Wang. Nobody seemed to know his given name. After siblings came along who were born to a different father, not even his mother had time for him anymore.

He had fine, limpid eyes, then, and to help support the family he went out as a child laborer to dig coal in a privately-owned mine. The entrance to the mine's coal pit was no wider than a winnowing fan and the miners went down to their toil wearing hardly a stitch of clothing. They dragged the coal one basketful at a time, crawling on all fours and holding a carbide lamp with their mouths. Once when they were trying to remove an unexploded charge it detonated, blinding the boy in both eyes, and in that condition he returned to town. By the time I came to know him, he had groped his way in darkness for many years.

In those days the children of the town's poor had a side job of collecting manure. Everyone had a curved bamboo scoop and carried a basket over his shoulder. In their free time, children ventured into the fields and highways in search of excrement. Since many of the vehicles traveling the roads then were horse-drawn carts, a line of horse-droppings, stretched out like an ellipsis, was a common sight. It was not out of patriotic concern for public health that kids undertook this work, but simply to earn a little money. Every family had its own septic pool—there were no public toilets. At the spring sowing and autumn planting, farmers from the countryside would make the rounds, each carrying two buckets on a shoulder pole. They were shopping for shit, and at each home they'd produce a long ladle to stir and sample what was in a family's septic pool, appraising it as dense or watery and offering on that basis a price that ranged from six cents to eight cents for two bucketfuls.

In general, a household could not excrete very many bucketfuls in the course of a year and children went out collecting in order to make up the balance of what was needed. They tended to seek out the dung of herbivores, which was clean and odorless. They didn't care whether it was an effective fertilizer as long as they could mix it in with the rest and meet their quota. But the kids gathering dung were very numerous, while the excretory powers of draft-animals were finite, and it came to pass that some children toiled all day to bring home barely a few dozen pellets of sheep-scat. Others followed behind cattle, alert for the crucial moment when a cow raised its tail: they would scoot close, holding out their baskets to catch the poop in mid-air. Sometimes fights broke out as kids contended for the prize.

But there was a shortcut to success in this business, and that was to cultivate a relationship with the men who worked at the coach station. When they took a cart out to the countryside, if they'd let you go as an assistant, every time the horse pooped along the way you could jump down and rake it quickly into your basket. They wouldn't stop for you, but the carts moved slow enough that you could sprint to catch up and clamber back on board. On a round trip you could often fill your basket with the proceeds, and then enjoy some free time.

Brother Blind Man did odd jobs at the coach station: he cut the horses' fodder, fed them, and swept out the stables. Although he couldn't see, he was very careful in his work and knew each horse's temperament like the back of his hand.

Our family had not yet become so poor as to need me to gather manure. I wanted a harmonica, however, and my mother thought this was only a toy and refused to buy it for me. My grandmother encouraged me to earn the necessary money myself, and I could think of no other, or at any rate no simpler, way to do that than to sell manure. I began roving the streets after school in search of dung and enjoyed various pastimes with the urchins I joined in this quest.

On our street, the only grown-up whom the kids could get to know was Brother Blind Man. One rainy day they all made a plan to steal dung at the coach station, and my part in the scheme was to distract Brother Blind Man with chit-chat so he wouldn't notice what was going on. It didn't work. I couldn't tell whether his hearing was exceptionally good or his psychological intuition acute, but our childish tricks didn't fool him. Yet he didn't take it seriously and only rebuked us with a laugh, and he didn't really try to stop us. Though I thus started out as a duplicitous agent, in time I became his little pal. Maybe he was lonely. He was often quite willing to chat, taking a liking to me without ever having seen my face. Each Sunday when the station-hands were dispatching a cart, he'd bring me over to the driver and say, "Things aren't easy for this scrawny kid, so take him along, OK? He just wants to buy a harmonica."

This was during the Cultural Revolution. My father had served as District Head in this place since Liberation, and now he was regularly dragged in under guard to be publicly denounced and excoriated. Brother Blind Man had a great deal of decency and kindness; perhaps he felt that the multitude of his misfortunes and deprivations had simply been his fate, for he never complained about them. Seeing my family brought low only made him feel sorry for me.

They say it's harder to be made blind than to be born that way, because you know what you're missing. He had seen everything and had mental images—beautiful or otherwise—for every word.

Growing up under grinding constraint, as a child he had seldom had anything to say and passed for a blockhead. Now that he was blind he was voluble, and earning his own keep had helped him develop serenity. Many a rainy day he'd shoot the breeze with me in the shed where they prepared the horses' fodder, and unlike the drivers (who were fond of dirty stories) he didn't seem interested in women.

It was around that time that he made his way surreptitiously up the street to ask Wizard Zhu to instruct him in the arts of fortunetelling, and thereafter in free moments he would practice reciting mysterious rhymed gibberish. When I asked why he was learning this stuff, he said, "So I'll be able to scrounge a living."

"Aren't you making a living now?" I asked. He said he might live a few more decades, but the station for horse-drawn vehicles wasn't going to be around much longer, and what would he do when there were no horses to feed? You see, even then—amidst the chaos of that time—he could see into the future and was preparing a fallback. He didn't want to ever depend on anyone for a handout.

I pestered him a few times to tell my fortune, and he'd scoff that that was all fake and I shouldn't believe in it. If it's fake, I said, then aren't you cheating people? He explained that in this world there are always some who have reached an impasse in their lives and need to buy consolation for a few pennies . . . "and we the disabled, we're people too and we need to make a living somehow. Like they say: Heaven creates man, Heaven must provide him a livelihood. When our ancestors invented these tricks, it was to leave us a mouthful of rice."

"Come on," I said, "You've still got to tell my fortune," and—unable to keep putting me off—he ran his fingers carefully over my bones and looked thoughtful for a moment. Then he made a joke of it. "Sure, kid, your fortune's great! Don't worry about what your family's going through now. Henceforth acres of fine farmland shall be yours in abundance, and throngs of wives and concubines." I knew nothing about prognosticating from a person's bone structure; I thought he was just clowning around and badgered him to tell me my fortune for real by casting my horoscope.

"Let me tell you a story," he said. "In the Qing Dynasty there was a high official named Zhang Zhidong who was the equivalent of a provincial governor.[90] When he came to Hubei to take charge, he saw fortune-tellers all over the streets and surmised this was why the place was so backward. He intended to ban them. Being an educated man, however, he knew he couldn't just impose his will but needed to convince people, so he came incognito and sought out a blind man who would feel his bones. The blind man felt from his foot as far as his shoulder and pushed him away with a grunt. 'Dog's bones, that's what you've got. What do *you* need a reading for?' Zhang Zhidong gloated inwardly: *That's all I need to put you frauds out of business; am I not a dignified official of the highest rank? Yet you say I've the bones of a dog.* But he suggested mildly, 'All the same, Sir, why not finish your examination?'

"'What do you think I'm gonna find,' the fortune-teller growled, 'You got the head of a shining dragon on top o' these dog's bones?' But he resumed probing with his hands, and when he reached the crown of the head he fell to his knees with a thump, crying, 'Spare my life, Your Excellency. In truth, a dragon's head atop the bones of a dog. You must be some kind of a Lord.'

"Zhang Zhidong shrugged, speechless, and walked away. And so they let this guild of ours go on making a living."

Brother Blind Man's story astonished me, callow youth that I was, and naturally it only made me more importunate that he tell my fortune. "I can't tell your fortune," he said. "My Master explained that there are some people whose fortunes you just can't tell." I asked why that was so, and he said, "When you grow up you'll understand these things. You're still young; please, whatever you do, don't believe in this stuff. You'll find that all through life your fortune changes according to your state of mind, like the water in a stream: where the banks are far apart, the water flows smooth, but when the stream is narrow it rushes violently. Nothing's set in stone. As long as your character is good, why should you fret because you have no prospects?"

I probably didn't understand much of what he'd said, and I was downcast at his refusal. As I started to leave, he seemed to prick up his ears, listening to check whether anyone was around. Then he took my dustpan into the stables, where he crammed it full of horse-droppings and warned, "Hurry home, now, and don't let anyone see."

That autumn I finally bought a harmonica for three yuan. When I went to play it for him, an expression of great happiness suffused his face. I wanted him to play it a little, too, but he adamantly refused: "No, no, my mouth is dirty, I don't want to make it dirty."

All long gone, now. The station for horse-drawn coaches shut down years ago and I have no way of knowing how Brother Blind Man may have made his quiet exit from a world that kept him destitute all his life. Nor can I guess where my harmonica is gathering dust, and in any case I doubt it could ever again produce the pure notes of the gaiety of youth. I have wandered far from home, and it is only in dreams now that I sometimes see Brother Blind Man standing at the end of the bridge in the gritty wind, swinging to a lonely beat the gleaming dark castanets that had been his Master's gift.

Su Jiaqiao, a Man Apart

I have often wondered what opportunities would await a person of my generation if he were transported into classical times. Even if highly educated, we would find admission into the privileged official class extremely difficult, but if we lacked the gumption to rebel, what alternatives would we have?

Ancient texts suggest the good life could take two forms: individuals of a radical disposition could follow in the path of the wandering sages, while those more conservatively inclined could join the staff of a high official. The wandering sages pursued the reformation of society, or something close to it, and risked paying a high price for following their conscience. The officials, in the main, preserved the status quo, and though their lives were materially secure they had to show deference and obedience. That is to say, if a person was not unconcerned about losing his life but prized his integrity, neither of these paths was right for him.

For such a one, the ancient world devised a third way besides that of the sage and that of the functionary: the way of the hermit.

China has always been rich in traditions about the eremitical life,[91] but one of them is quite wrong: the saying that "The greatest hermits are found at Court; the middle-ranking hermits are found in the bustling life of the city; and the least of the hermits make their homes in the mountains and the forests."[92] In my opinion, "hermits at Court" are nothing but sycophants with high IQs; "hermits in city life" are simply people of refinement; and the hermits of mountain and forest are the men who truly go their own way.

The designation "a man apart" derives from the 'Treading' hexagram of the *I Ching*.[93] "The Man Apart walks his equable way, and his steadfastness shall meet with good fortune." Kong Yingda unpacked this line as follows: "Because the man who remains apart in seclusion holds fast to what is right, he shall enjoy good fortune."[94] The point is that one should not be honored as a hermit merely for living alone in a desolate place: one must also hold fast to the Way and act with justice.

In our time, almost all the secluded places have been nationalized, so the objective conditions necessary to live in refined seclusion no longer exist. And yet the kind of man who lives in this world, but inwardly apart, has not yet become extinct. Of all my friends, Brother Su Jiaqiao most closely approaches this ideal.

❧

Su Jiaqiao entered college in 1980, two years after me. We had grown up together in the mountain town of Lichuan. Our fathers had been partners in the campaign to suppress the bandits, so you could say our friendship spanned generations.

At the start of the '80s there was still a macho tone to the Nationalities colleges[95] and a dozen or so of us whose fathers had known one another in Lichuan banded together to drink and read poetry. It didn't take much to turn us into a gang of toughs. We were a wild bunch that roamed with knives in our sleeves, and in my memories of college there is no shortage of flashing blades and bloodshed. There were big fights and little fights, we hurt and were hurt, and about the only feeling I have now for that chapter in my life is embarrassment.

Upon graduation I was assigned to the Board of Education in my hometown, and within two years our whole gang had similarly been dispatched to jobs in the boondocks. Brother Su was sent to the middle school in the little town of Tuanbao. As an Inspector of Schools I often toured the countryside making official visits. Soon after his arrival he had become the talk of teachers and students alike. The country schools then were all housed in rough-hewn wooden buildings where flimsy partitions, by no means soundproof, separated the staff bedrooms. The teachers complained that every night without fail he would regale them with an opus in three parts:

I) Drink, recite poetry, wax maudlin.

II) When the liquor runs out, pee into a bottle (the toilet was too far away).

III) Around midnight, hurl the bottle from his window. After it explodes, his neighbors can go to sleep.

He taught language and literature, and he taught extremely well. But he was not one to bother himself about the rules of his job. Many a time he was still asleep after the bell had rung for class. The student cadre would need to go knock at his door, and he'd scramble out of bed and hurry into the classroom without even washing his face, asking in a conspiratorial whisper, "What was I talking about last time?" Sometimes he was too hung over and would give the kids a study hall while he put his head down on the teacher's desk and slept. Once they heard snoring but on looking up couldn't see him. They mounted the teacher's platform and discovered Teacher Su had slid under the desk, wrapped in lovely dreams.

In the autumn of 1983 I went to see him with another member of our old gang and the three of us went out drinking and ended up lying wasted in the street. A few puzzled locals approached with a torch. One was a parent who cried out in dismay, "Teacher Su! Whatcha sleepin' here for?"

Brother Su blinked up into the light and waved them away with a chuckle: "All is well, kind Sir. You may return to your pursuits and engagements; after a short rest, we will be on our way." It brought to mind the line from Xin Qiji, *I pushed away the pine, 'Be off with you!'* [96]—for it was approximately the same situation. When we staggered off down the street, I fell into a sewer, but luckily the other two fished me out and took turns carrying me on their backs until we reached Su's dormitory where all three squeezed into his bed coated with slime—the term "filthy drunk" was seldom more apposite—and fell asleep in our clothes. The curious thing was that I went back to see him a month later and noticed the same sheets on his bed, still smeared all over with sewage, though that had long since dried. The stench was almost visible inside the room, like heat waves.

In those days he was a bachelor who had no peer for filth, sloth, and chaotic living. The administrator for the Tuanbao school hub made a formal complaint, so we had to transfer him to Wangying Middle School where he roomed with Fang Zhou, another one of our gang from college. I visited the two of them and found the floor covered with wine bottles. That evening when we sat down to drink, I noticed that when he opened a bottle he'd sniff it carefully; sometimes he'd close it up again and put it back down, other times he'd pour it into the drinking bowls. When I inquired, it turned out that some of the bottles were filled with urine and they hadn't got round yet to collecting and disposing of them. When we were all drunk and sleepy I was startled to find that these two chums shared the same basin for washing face, crotch, and feet; and possessing only a single toothbrush, they shared that too.

In 1984 we finally succeeded in setting him up with a kindly woman of good character who lived in the city of Enshi. She would later become his wife, but I remember the first time she came to meet him out in the countryside (changing buses more than once) and entered the room and caught sight of the bed with its filthy black sheets. There was nowhere else to sit, so she took the opportunity to strip the sheets, intending to wash them for him, and found this was only the top layer: there was another set of sheets, equally dirty, beneath them; and taking these off, she found another layer . . . five altogether, and it appeared that wild animals had made prolonged use of them on both sides. He giggled. Women had a certain refinement in those days, but, remarkably, she was not repelled; indeed, that very mat of rice straw eventually became their fragrant marriage bed.

❧

Allen Ginsberg, the American Beat poet, famously declared, "We're not our skin of grime: in our heart there has always bloomed a sunflower, holy and pure."[97] Had it not been for Su Jiaqiao's inner character, could this coarse-looking man who taught school in the countryside have won a fair woman's love?

Zhou Zuoren once said his student Fei Ming looked like a praying mantis. I don't get that feeling from old pictures of Fei Ming. But my friend Su Jiaqiao, in build and features, does bear a close resemblance to a grasshopper. In the countryside, we called him Jumping Chicken, because his hands and feet were elongated, his head rather small and thin, and his eyeballs protruded. If he removed the glasses he'd worn since childhood, he became the spitting image of Feng Gong.[98] He poked fun at himself: "I'm tall as a model and thin as a phone pole; my bones are light as a swallow's, and when the chorus claps, I can't help dancing; and my thick and lustrous hair is irresistible—to lice, anyway."

Su Jiaqiao loves to read and has a remarkable grasp of classical learning. Early on, he was partial to the literature of the Wei and Jin Dynasties, with the result that in speech and manner he came to resemble the worthies of the Bamboo Grove.[99] He oscillated between fierce resolution and abject despondency. Underneath his erratic behavior lay a sense of life's tragic quality and, with it, a gentle respect for others.

One evening shortly before New Year's, when the town was muffled in deep snow, I was walking home with him, slightly drunk, when we came upon an elderly beggar huddled on the pavement in front of an office building. Su Jiaqiao pulled me over to talk with the man, who told us the floods that year had washed away his house, and he had had no choice at year's end but to come into town and beg; his brief tale finished, he began to weep. The old man put us both in mind of the hard times of our childhood, and soon the three of us were all embracing one another tearfully in the street. We emptied our pockets of change and made obeisance as we said goodbye. This was China at the start of the '80s, when there still remained something of the old ways.

He had by then developed a distinctive style of teaching. The curriculum was full of essays by Liu Baiyu, Wei Wei, and Yang Shuo:[100] whenever he got to these lessons he belittled them and put the book aside. In its place he took out mimeographs of *The Peeled Date*, the samizdat magazine of our poetry club, and endeavored to expound to his students the beauties and subtleties therein. There reigned in his classroom what I call the pedagogy of the teahouse. Often he would draw the children into a free discussion where his only role was to stimulate their train of thought with occasional comments. This approach initially caused the head of the school some unease, and he could not help remonstrating with Teacher Su. No one expected that his students would come out on top in the rankings of the district examinations, year after year. When that started happening, people did a double-take and saw him in a new light.

Some years afterward, we went back to that rural district

and when we occasionally ran into former students (long since embarked on their lives) or locals without any connection to the schools, I noticed that they still treated him with deference, while he often could not remember their full names.

જ

Time passes quickly in the hill country. Back then we were a band of rascals who were crazy about poetry and spent much of our time getting blind drunk as we dreamt of literature, squandering our youth while deploring the world and its ways. Each weekend, all of us who taught school in the countryside would go into town to dine together. We'd cut the mimeograph[101] of our underground poetry magazine and share whatever gems we'd encountered in our reading that week, and we would hold debates very much in the style of the Jixia Academy.[102] Late one summer night under a full moon, when the ill-lit streets were empty and the drinking had reached its height, Su Jiaqiao proposed that we walk naked through town in a revival of the ancient practice of *xingsan:* people of the Wei and Jin dynasties, when taking medicines that generated almost unbearable internal heat, found it necessary to rush about naked in order to release that heat. So we all strolled downtown wearing hardly a stitch of clothing. When pale white bodies bobbed tipsily through the streets, the few people who caught a glimpse of us must have shuddered in the belief that they were seeing, once more upon this earth, a troop of the dead in the care of a Tujia corpse-driver.[103]

When we were thus practicing *xingsan*, we were usually pretty drunk. In those days my friends and I were a bit on the wild side and did a lot of mischief. If we saw a wooden signboard hanging in front of an official building, Su Jiaqiao and I would angrily take it down and carry it off at a brisk run till we found an out-of-the-way place to dump it. One time we only noticed *after* dumping a sign that its imposing inscription was PEOPLE'S COURT, and we laughed uproariously, "Better not mess with *them*!" We hurried back panting with the sign and hung it up again.

In those days it was a three-day bus ride to the provincial capital. Our only connection with the world outside the mountains was reading. Our passion for reading let us keep pace with the gradual opening-up that was then unfolding. We knew that our poetry club, there in the remote hill country, was part of a flowering of associations devoted to the New Literature.[104] How we longed to escape the mountains that hemmed us round! In the winter of 1984, word came of a recruiting drive for the great Northwest: there would be no background checks.[105] I resolved to head west, out through the sunny pass.[106] On hearing of this, Su Jiaqiao feared that if I were alone it would be dangerous to make the journey and hard for me to return, so he went home and started packing, prepared to leave without saying goodbye to his family. Alas, on account of my family's interference I did not set out and we never made good our escape.

In 1988, I earned my second degree and was assigned to work on Hainan. Returning to the hill country to say my goodbyes, I learned that Teacher Su was being transferred to a technical school in Enshi. He therefore set out with me

A PASSAGE TO HAINAN

on the first leg of my journey from Lichuan, but 'passing his own door'[107] he stayed with me and we hitched a ride on a truck to Wuhan. Judging that it would be tedious for me to travel the long remainder of the journey alone, he stuck with me for the train ride to Zhanjiang, but then, deciding he couldn't bear to see me go off alone into the distance, he chose also to endure the bumpy ride to Hai'an, and finally, for the hell of it, sailed across to Haikou with me, and only then—the next day—did he set out alone on the long journey back. In those days, neither one of us had any money to spare, and this friendly gesture bespoke a deep affection, as sure as the thousand fathoms of Peach Blossom Pond.[108]

❧

Su Jiaqiao's critical solitude arose from his family background. His father and mine were both the sons of small landholders, and finding themselves at Enshi when power changed hands, they joined the first entering class at Revolution U., graduated together, and were both assigned to Lichuan during the campaign to suppress the bandits of Wendou, Shaxi, and Changshun Townships. Su *père* was District Magistrate while my father was Party Secretary. During the Cultural Revolution, Su's father was the local manager of the People's Bank and his mother was a cadre at the grocery co-op. In a pattern tragically repeated in many other families of that era, his father was identified as a 'capitalist-roader' and singled out for humiliation and struggle sessions,[109] while his mother took her stand in the 'rebel faction' on the other side.

These artificial political distinctions nearly broke his family apart. His elder brother and sister had already been dispatched to the countryside, but he—only a few years old—was left to watch his parents rage at each other every day and by turns be "struggled against." For the reality of the Cultural Revolution was not at all that the rebel faction was always on top, nor did that faction consist solely of those who were out to beat, smash, and loot. Most of the rebel-faction people could be called the "angry right-wingers" of their day[110] whose abiding resentment of social injustice made them quick to heed the Leader's call to defy the bureaucracy. During the "Cultural Revolution," it was very often the rebel faction that was beaten down and punished.

While his mother was away carrying on the Revolution, Su Jiaqiao spent his days in the care of his unfortunate and alcoholic father who, each time he anesthetized himself, would sit the boy down across from him and considerately pour a drink for him, too. Thus the lad learned very young what drinking is about, and what it is for. During those intervals when the father was restored to his post, he became very busy and the boy had to be trundled off to live with his mother in the peasant village where she had been sent. The parents lived apart but did not divorce since neither could bear to abandon the child.

Thus he grew up quietly in a chaotic time, watching his parents attack each other and seeing one parent or the other become subject to persecution each time the authorities changed their tune. He had no way to judge which points of view were right or wrong among the older generation, but gradually he came to see clearly what was good and evil in society. After he began working, he tried to bridge the gulf which history had set between his parents (both retired now), and with his siblings he managed to persuade them to live once more under the same roof, though still not together, for the old couple would not speak to each other. His mother faded away in the depression that had haunted her most of her life. His father developed an intermittent dementia, and this man who had preserved his dignity for so long now often couldn't remember anything, or he'd imagine

himself back in the Red Terror and cry, *They're coming to arrest me again, hide me, hide me somewhere, quick!* Those of the
older generation who had endured class struggle in middle
age were subject to these flashbacks of persecution for the
rest of their lives.

By this time Su Jiaqiao, having a wife and child, had
started working for the People's Bank in Enshi City, and he
had to find time to take care of his father too. In senility the
old man was like a retarded child, liable to urinate at any
time, anywhere, at home or in the courtyard of his work
unit. Witnessing the indignities to which old age is reduced,
Su Jiaqiao was pained and embarrassed and often remarked
to me that if he himself should begin to lose his dignity in
old age he would kill himself for sure. Sometime after that,
during one of his occasional intervals of lucidity, the father
returned alone to Lichuan—alone in all his frailty—and with
great dignity jumped into the Qing River. Like my father, he
never talked about his family's history and never went back
to his native town. These children of 'the exploiting class,'
who threw themselves wholeheartedly into the Revolution
. . . how many of them, after their families were shattered,
buried their chilling memories in silence.

Su Jiaqiao had an older sister who was like a mother to
him and had been one of the prettiest girls in Lichuan. In
the chaos of the C.R. she lost her chance for education and
was sent to the countryside, where at a young age she married an educated youth from Wuhan. Eventually this fellow
returned to the city, leaving her with a young son in the
mountains. She remarried—a worker this time—and when
the plant shut down, husband and wife both found them-

selves unemployed.[111] One winter day she died of carbon-monoxide poisoning, probably without even realizing it was happening. Her eldest son, who with plenty of firm guidance from all of us had grown up as a good kid, later became a gang member. After getting entangled in a vendetta, he was charged with homicide and went to prison.

❧

Su Jiaqiao had majored in Chinese literature, but after this train of sorrows he became, of all things, a bank accountant and gradually settled down into middle age. The bank manager had once been his father's protégé. Most of Su's classmates from college had achieved prominence in the prefecture. He alone insisted on staying out of the Party, indeed staying out of any group. In the boom times he kept his humble place, making a quiet living from his skill with figures. Today he has more seniority than any other employee at that bank. He goes his own way, and never curries favor with the boss. Working at the bank is not without benefits: fresh fruit and vegetables are often divvied up, but on these occasions he hangs back and lets the others pick out what they want. If there's anything left, he may take something home.

He refuses to enter into this world's struggles, and his magnanimous and easy-going disposition has naturally made him the eccentric fellow of whom everyone is rather fond. As a joke, they sometimes address him as Manager, even in the presence of the real manager, whose loud bureaucratic tone he then imitates as he grants their requests. The boss knows him well enough to take no offense, and his colleagues seem to admire him, wistfully, for being so detached from the system.

A hangover can put him in a playful mood at lunchtime, and he may invite executives to sit with him in the cafeteria. He then archly asks: "I suppose you're all Party members?" Not quite sure where this is leading, the executives nod. Then he asks whether they have read the *Communist Manifesto* and *Das Kapital*. Awkwardly, they shake their heads. "Well, then," he laughs, "I'll give you a Communist Party in-service lecture." Thinking he's a bit of a clown, they don't take it seriously, but they do listen—since they're there, after all—as he pours out one story after another, from Marx and Engels through the Comintern and Lenin's *State and Revolution*, explaining the difference between the Bolsheviks and the Trotskyists, comparing Stalin and Mao . . . until the managers are dumbfounded.

This is the kind of man he is, with an odd face and shabby clothes, barreling in and out of the office with his prominent eyes not really focused on anything. Yet whenever the bank's national headquarters needs to form a team of writers for an important document to be drafted in Beijing, the staff in his district usually recommend him unanimously. At first, he didn't want to do it, but after I pointed out that if he came to Beijing we could go drinking together, he made the trip several times. Some officials in the capital were impressed by his talent and asked whether he'd consider leaving the hill country to take a more significant post. Most men would have seen in such an offer the answer to their prayers, but his spirit is like the grassland where nothing impure can grow.

He had always admired the celebrated remark of Zhang Han:[112] *That life alone is noble which is in accord with one's deepest desires. Why should I go a thousand miles to wheedle a name and a title?* And so he returned to the hill country with a hearty laugh, and went back to being a low-level civil servant.

Zhuangzi says that in the mountain forests there is but one kind of timber that survives, and it survives because it doesn't fit into any utilitarian categories.[113] It doesn't get chopped down to supply the palace with a ridgepole, for example, because it's not that tall and fine; but neither does it get cut for firewood, because it's not a tangle of worthless growth. This kind of tree can survive in a dangerous world and live out the years which Heaven has allotted it. It is from this passage that *san*, 'diffuse, unclassifiable', came to be part of a word for 'hermit', *sanren*. In just this sense, Su Jiaqiao's nature was unclassifiable and untangled. Fame, rank, and wealth were to him no more than clouds floating past.[114] He had freed himself of all desire for worldly validation.

&

Not so for the ordinary person living a social life: fame and wealth bind him like chains. A person of refinement may keep clear of greed, but it is not so easy to purify oneself of the yearning for validation. You can renounce the world, but then you will harbor the dream of perfecting yourself as a monk and being recognized as one far advanced in the Way. How much more entangled, then, the ordinary folk who are in thrall to the seven passions and the six desires!

The man of detachment has not, to be sure, erased from his heart every trace of love and hatred. But he will not devote those impulses of his spirit to procuring badges of achievement and fame.

His small house contains one of the few notable book collections in western Hubei; his literary learning runs deep. He keeps his formidable writing talent under a bushel. It is true that he was the first of our gang to make his presence felt, albeit with a low profile, on the Internet, and it was his influence, as well as that of Shicun and Qing Chen,[115] that drew me back to writing, especially writing of the polemical kind. Yet he tends to exercise his influence through conversation, and in this age where so much is for show he has never submitted anything for publication. He never puts on airs, and even today, very few people know who he is.

He is at home in a variety of styles both new and old. The elegant, dry wit of his essays echoes Feng Zikai,[116] and his grounding in ancient poetry and the lyric forms is most unusual. He mixes sardonic humor with a restrained satire, evoking the cloak-and-rapier flair of Nie Gannu and Yang Xianyi.[117] When I was behind bars, he once sent me a letter composed in the meter of a Song-Dynasty lyric:[118]

In the long time since we were parted, I have missed you.
I light a cigarette, hang a lantern, and sit disconsolate,
Sipping a cup of hard white liquor:
'Tis a cold wind and strong that blows down the river.
I wonder whether you have warm clothes.
I'm worried, I'm just worried,
About a Du Fu[119] who is poor and thin.

Years have passed since we separated;
When shall we meet again?
Once or twice you came back, Brother,
And I wished to speak with you,
But you left too soon.
Thoughts of the past leave me at a loss.

How fares my brother, are you well?
When a letter comes from you, I read it several times.
Don't tell me to let it go.
I can imagine you leaning alone on a railing,
Loath to recall how we used to carouse.
Remember we are friends through life and death.
In the old town I'm keeping a parcel of land for you.
Once your affairs are sorted out, you'll come back,
And you and I will care for each other again.

&

For years I used to wring my hands over the waste of this man's talent and virtue, buried in the hill country. Now I am beginning to understand the fulfillment he may have found in his way of life. From of old, scholars have felt torn between conflicting desires to go out into the world and to remain detached from it. Most of them went out into the world, failed, and only then chose the path of a reclusive scholar. But Su Jiaqiao renounced all worldly striving from the beginning, in his youth, and chose a way of life that was eremitical but had no conventions to define it.

In others' eyes, he has carried independence of thought and action to an extreme verging on impropriety. Among the three million inhabitants of the prefecture, there's hardly anyone he can talk to. Only when a few of his scattered friends go back for a reunion will he hold an animated and festive conversation all night long, beating the wine-kettle and drinking it dry. Usually he devotes the early morning and the late evening to lonely walks through his city in the hills. Threading his way through town, over the years he has noted the gradual disappearance of the old houses built in the local style, and he feels keenly the loss of the alleys of his childhood. At these times he stands helpless amid the city's vulgar din as if stunned and trying to recall what was once dear to him.

Once he was a fan of Lu Xun, but now he says he likes Hu Shih better.[120] Back when I was a fierce partisan for the cause of liberty, he used to tell me that tolerance was more important than freedom. He did his best to meet this world with a smile, and to old classmates who had become officials he would patiently explain the meaning of democracy. Even when encountering an old friend who had entered the Party in middle age, he kept his mockery gentle: "An oath of loyalty is indeed solemn and sacred . . . but only if you actually believe in it."

There is a poem of Su Shi that says, "Having no business to attend to, the hermit does not venture forth; but once in a while on a lovely evening he will chase the east wind." But Su Jiaqiao likes to go out every day, walking in the open country. The year before last he suffered a couple of falls, breaking first one leg and then the other. This led him to take up bicycling with gusto. Apart from work, he passes all his time either on the bike or beside the wine-jar. Like me, he has retained the habit of drinking alone and often manages to get himself drunk. When friends tease him and ask what happened to all his ideals, he answers with a smile, "It's enough if my boss doesn't yell at me every day." The truth is that everyone in his circle holds him in considerable, even if undemonstrative, respect. In this vapid era, truly interesting human beings are rare. Alone in the mountains, Su Jiaqiao has kept up with the times but maintains a critical distance. He casts a cold eye on this raucous and unhinged epoch of prosperity, for the glory and honor of this world inspire in him only a kind of disdain.

Yet every day he goes online and engages in a little discussion on Weibo[121] as if he wished to maintain a polite connection with this world. I know full well that his heart is not in it—his thoughts are far away, as if he had moved to an unattainable distance whence he observes us with amusement. His most recent post on Weibo was as follows:

A bit of sun today. Biked to the outskirts of town. Gazed upon a distant hill wreathed in mist. Recited a verse by Tao Hongjing, here shared with 'Net friends:

What's in the hills?
Only an abundance of white clouds over the ridge;
They are my solitary delight, and nothing more.
I can't take hold of them and present them to Your Lordship.[122]

Su Shi asks: "Can any see the hermit passing by, elusive as the shadow of a lonely swan?"[123] When I recall this line,

I think of Su Jiaqiao blending into the crowd in his native town, where no one even knows his face.

Tomb Lantern
Fragmentary memories of my Grandmother

Not until 1983, when 21 years old, did I grasp the meaning of death.

Of all my kin, my maternal grandmother had showed me the greatest affection and exercised a profound influence. She left me abruptly one autumn day when her 78-year-long journey of hardship had reached its end. For years thereafter I remained sunk in a grief from which it was hard to extricate myself.

At Lichuan, a town on the western edge of Hubei, she was interred with dignity according to the rites of the Tujia people. As she was buried on the hillside behind the high school, anthems of praise floated above the reverent trill of the pipes. A *feng shui* consultant had directed that the head of her grave point northeast toward the lowlands where she'd been born. She had always wanted to return there, to the plain between the Yangtze and the Han, but now would never go back there alive.

In those days it was still the Tujia custom that, for seven weeks after the burial, a kinsman should bring a lantern to the tomb each night and leave it burning there. This was to cast a ray of light upon the long dark road which the deceased must travel. The nature of that gloomy corridor and what kind of world lay beyond it are things I still have no way to know. My father was, nominally, a cadre—he had

123

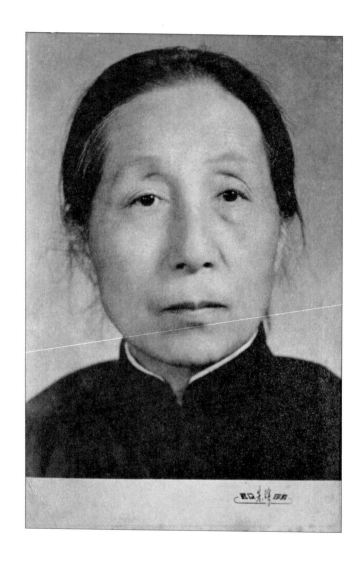

Cheng Fenglin, *date unknown*

been rehabilitated not long before—and was skittish about publicly observing a practice that could have been taken as evidence of superstition. I on the other hand was anxious about the journey that Grandmother faced alone, and each day as twilight fell I lit an oil lamp and made my way sadly to the slope where monuments clustered like a grove, and set a tomb lantern for her there. I wasn't convinced that death was a journey of no return, and while I knelt alone to burn joss paper and light firecrackers at her grave, and then prostrated myself in tears, the idea did not entirely leave me that I might wake Grandmother from a deep sleep. When I pressed my ear to the freshly-dug earth I had a childish fantasy that I would hear her groaning from inside the coffin and would claw away the rocks and mud with my fingers to rescue the person who, of all those near and dear to me, was irreplaceable.

The tomb lantern flickered soundlessly in the evening breeze as lights came on, one after another, in the bleak little town below. I sat high up the hillside among the dead and looked down on the living, too young to penetrate the mystery. Each time I returned reluctantly from Grandmother's grave in the last of the twilight, I would steal backward glances at the tiny spark of the lantern, concerned that it might have gone out. I needed it to go on illumining this place where she had never been at home and was now swallowed up in night. And even more, I needed it to shed light on my own path which seemed so dark now that she was gone.

❧

Grandmother was born in 1905 to a middle-class family in Tian'erhe township, Hanchuan county. She was the eldest daughter, named Cheng Fenglin. Everyone in the family called her Brother Fenglin.[124] When she was only a few years old, her mother died of an illness. Her father, an educated man, had his heart set on studying in Japan, so he sent her to be raised by one of her mother's sisters at Wuxue. My great-grandfather studied law for eight years at Waseda University and when he came back from Japan the Republican government appointed him chief justice of the high court of Gansu Province. Grandmother's childhood and teenage years passed in private schooling, and she was released at a fairly early age from foot-binding, but the instep of her feet, having once been broken, remained somewhat deformed. In some manner that is not now clear to me, her early life was marked by neglect or maltreatment. I recall that when I was little, whenever she spoke of her childhood her old eyes would fill with tears.

Around age 23 her father betrothed her to the third son of the Lius, a privileged family of Ganyi township in Tianmen County. Mr. Liu, Senior, had retired from his career as a magistrate in Shangshui County, Henan, and built himself an imposing mansion in Ganyi. His eldest son went into trade, the second boy found work in textiles, and the third— my maternal grandfather, Liu Jilü—graduated as a sergeant in the eighth class to pass through Whampoa. The fourth son, Liu Jilin, would later join the underground Communist Party and study in the Soviet Union. He became a scholar who is honored today as the nation's pre-eminent scientific expert on corn. We called him Fourth Great-Uncle.

The alliance of the Liu and Cheng families may have arisen from the friendship of the patriarchs, but the two clans were well-matched socially and politically. As he prepared to take his second wife and their son to his post in a distant province, Great-Grandfather felt some affection for his motherless daughter and wanted to entrust her to a reliable person. He had no idea that in a country where war and chaos were about to become the norm, his choice would have tragic and lasting repercussions. This must have been their fate.

Grandmother moved into the Liu compound and gave birth about a year later to my mother, whom Grandfather named Liu Lingyun[125]—a name expressive of the high hopes that a modern military man entertained for his child. With the exception of the patriarch himself, almost all the Liu men had thrown themselves into the struggle that was unfolding in the outside world, and the family still living in the manor consisted of women and children. As to whether my grandmother tasted the joy of the newly-married, and whether Grandfather ever managed to slip away from his wars and make a tender visit to his wife, Mother never talked about those things and there's no way to know now. But Grandmother never had another child, and we can infer that when she endured various hardships to raise my mother she was passing her life in a kind of waiting, like a woman leaning in a doorway.

To this day my grandfather's life has remained shrouded in mystery. Neither my grandmother nor my mother would talk about it. Only years after they passed on did I begin to glimpse an outline, first from a newly-compiled genealogy of the Liu clan and then from reminiscences shared by relatives. During the years of my own crisis, a few older alumni of Whampoa approached me with offers of assistance but it turned out they hadn't known my grandfather; they were just kindly disposed toward me because they knew of him and honored him as their senior. All I could find out was that Grandfather had once served as an officer in Chiang Kai-shek's bodyguard: in the Liu manor there had hung a photo of him in his dress uniform standing behind the Generalissimo. During the War Against Japan he was chief of staff at the headquarters of General Qiu Qingquan.[126] When Hubei was recovered from the Japanese, he seems to have taken command of Wuhan as a major-general. In 1948 he was sent as commander and magistrate to Enshi in western Hubei. He disembarked and went ashore at Badong, but riding in his Jeep through Jianshi County he was ambushed in a defile by a group that has never been clearly identified.

From 1927 till 1945, people all over China were separated by war and the land did not know a single day of peaceful governance. Most of the rich and prominent families were wiped out in the course of struggles that pitted party against party, class against class, or nation against nation, and the Liu clan was no exception. After Great-Grandfather passed away, each branch of the family (and they already had separate kitchens and budgets) grew farther apart. Grandmother didn't receive any support from Grandfather and had to support herself by picking cotton, spinning yarn, and mending people's clothes. She was sure that her husband would come back and her eighteen years of faithful waiting would be rewarded with a blissful reunion in a time of peace. But when peace came, dreadful news was brought to her: thinking his wife and daughter must have perished amid the disasters of war, he had remarried in Chongqing and now had two sons. My mother made an uproar that brought obloquy upon him, and he was censured by his Party, so Grandfather had to come back and demand a divorce from Grandmother. She refused to take any compensation from him and chose to leave his position, reputation, and new family intact. After putting her fingerprint on the divorce papers, she fainted.

The whole Liu clan knew the virtue of Third Brother's Wife and there was no lack of condemnation for his heartlessness, but that didn't do her any good. They all urged her to keep on living in the Manor, which was now practically in ruins, and she began to live out her long widowhood. When Grandfather was gunned down and his body was brought to Wuhan, Grandmother escorted the casket without a trace of bitterness and had him interred in the burial-ground at the Manor. She seems to have chosen to remain forever a daughter-in-law of the Liu clan. She waited upon a young maid whom Great-Grandfather had taken as the last of his concubines. (The girl, though younger than herself, was called her "mother-in-law.") And she often helped out the fourth of the Liu brothers, who was at that time an impecunious student and the only uncle my mother had.

♥っ

Thanks to her skills as a seamstress and her frugal way of life, Grandmother was able to support my mother till she finished high school in Wuhan, at which point Mother came back to the countryside and taught school, thus sharing the burden which Grandmother had long borne alone. This was the year Hubei came under Communist control, and Mother decided to take the entrance exam for Revolution U. Upon graduation, to her surprise she was dispatched to Enshi in western Hubei, deep in the mountains, precisely where her detested father had met his doom. This development caused Grandmother great anxiety, but there was nothing she could do to hold her headstrong daughter back.

During Land Reform, Grandmother was classified as a poor handicraft-worker and joined the tailors' union in town. Mother married my father in Lichuan at a dangerous time, the period of counterinsurgency and land reform. Grandmother had no wish to leave her native place for the hill country, and those out-of-the-way locales with strange names doubtless stirred in her heart an anguish that she could not put into words. But as her only daughter, my mother felt she could not leave Grandmother to face widowhood alone and far away. My older sister was about to be born and Grandmother's help was needed: when it was put to her like that, Grandmother could not refuse. She sailed upriver to Wanxian[127] and from there made her way on foot to Wangying District in Lichuan, the village called West Brook—for there, in that unspeakably barren and remote mountain valley, my parents were assigned to the ironworks. Grandmother arrived on the scene like a savior. There was little joy, and much hardship and humiliation, to be shared by joining her daughter. At that time my family was living in a cave, and this was where Grandmother acted as midwife at my sister's birth. Soon after, Mother was branded a Rightist, and malicious tongues denounced these two women as the wife and daughter of a warlord. This was the taint that caused them tribulation for the rest of their lives. In the midst of my mother's troubles, my second sister was born premature, and this was during the time that would be called the three years of "natural disasters."[128] She was not quite four pounds, and both Father and Mother thought it too difficult to keep her alive. But Grandmother would not let them give up on her and fed her mouthfuls of rice water, one at a time, till this infant at death's door began to grow. In those days the acute shortage of grains menaced even adults with famine: Grandmother drew on her experiences of surviving disaster to help our family endure yet another of the world's calamities. Swollen with edema, she dragged herself out onto the undeveloped hillsides and hoed a bit of barren ground, planting seeds in the hope of survival; and the evening meals she boiled from those coarse cereals seemed sumptuous to our family of five and remained the most warm and fragrant memory of the time we lived in a cave.

Father needed a son who would love what he had loved and hate what he had hated, and Mother, though humiliated by Reform Through Labor Under Supervision, managed to bear him a son: not me, but my older brother who died young. After only a few months he was killed when an incompetent village doctor gave him an injection. Lacking any way to give vent to his rage, my father precipitated a family crisis and my strong-willed mother almost left him. Once again, it was Grandmother with her kindly wisdom who stepped in to soothe my mother: "As I see it, this man has a violent temper but a good heart." Indeed, does any good quality rank higher than a good heart? Kindness was important to her. She had an innate kindness which she steadfastly maintained, and it was this virtue of hers that proved the salvation of my imperiled family. And so in 1962 I made my vociferous entrance into this world.

I am told the sun was dazzling that midsummer morning. Grandmother cut my umbilical cord with a scissors and washed the blood from me. Father laughed gaily to hear my vigorous crying, and Mother wept tears mixing grief and joy. I became Grandmother's favorite, but for my parents I would prove a lifelong source of heartache.

❦

When I was two, the ironworks which my father had been sent to manage finally shut down after using up all the local timber for fuel, bringing its historic mission to an ignominious close.[129] He was dispatched to take charge of a coal mine at Qiyue Mountain, while Mother was assigned to the grocery co-op in Wangying District. Grandmother made the move with us three children into the small streets of the old town. My first childhood memories are of that house on stilts by the river.

Thus did I grow, carried about with her in her arms, and every night I would hug those chapped feet which had been warped by foot-binding, falling asleep to the sound of her nursery rhymes. Grandmother had once studied at a private school and had read many of the classic dramas, and she could recite poetry with the authentic intonation. To this day I distinctly recall that typically Tujia wood-frame house, propped up somewhat askew on the bank of a small tributary in the upper reaches of the Qing River. Outside the window stood a *cailang*, a balcony, and when I peed from that *cailang* I could hit the cormorant boat moored below. Across the river was a little village called Zhuanzhuan Tian, and the sounds of the farmers threshing their grain often accompanied Grandmother's musical recitation of poetry, giving me early on an intuitive grasp of rhythm and rhyme.

The little town had no electricity then, and the oil lamps in the old house swayed subtly in the manner of a Tang Dynasty poem. Repeatedly I'd ask to hear stories from the *Twenty-four Paragons,* of which I never tired,[130] and Grandmother would get choked up as she told the tales; my childhood was perhaps more emotionally susceptible than most, and the two of us would often soak our pillow-covers with tears. If I know anything of, and have some feel for, classical literature and art, it is wholly due to Grandmother's early instruction. The spoken dramas of folk literature resonated with her personal experience and quivered with grief in her retelling.

The town's weakest and most disadvantaged inhabitants seemed to be clustered on the lane where we dwelt. At the head of the block, on the left, were the four orphans of the

Xiong family whose parents had committed suicide. On the right lived Chen the mute with his aged mother. In the middle was Grannie Kuang, the landlord's wife, and Old Lady Hu, who was ninety and qualified for welfare.[131] There was also a disabled couple who lived with their daughter. In the old wood house next door there were Grannie Huang and her husband, and Uncle Kaifu the horse-trader. Comparatively speaking, we could have been considered a rich and powerful family.

And though we were outsiders, thanks to Grandmother's decency and kindness we were quickly accepted into this humble society, winning the respect of everyone on the street. At one time or another that year, every family ran short of rice or fuel, and countless times they came looking for "Grandma" to help them out—and that is what they called her. She was the first to teach me the meaning of kindness. After she had me take some food down the street to a beggar, I began—and this probably had not been her plan—I began bringing beggars home whenever I encountered them. I was too young to understand how limited were our own family's means, but Grandmother was always pleased with my childish philanthropy. After a while my mother couldn't stand the strain on our finances (for beggars were numerous in those days) and put her foot down, which made me cry with frustration and hurt, but Grandmother remained encouraging and supportive and that made all the difference.

I had learned many characters before the age of five and could recite quite a few classic poems, and this was entirely due to Grandmother's tutelage. To bring in extra money, Grandmother started quietly working as a seamstress, making or mending the neighbors' clothes. If they had any money, they'd give a little; if they didn't, they'd voice their thanks, and Grandmother never demanded payment. Once she was so busy she got confused and gave me the wrong medicine when I was suffering from intestinal parasites, and I fell down foaming at the mouth. Grandmother scooped me up and did her best to run on her hobbled feet to the hospital downtown. When the doctors revived me, her eyes had become red and swollen.

Because of her, I think by the age of four I had tasted all the happiness that was to be mine in this life. For then came the Cultural Revolution, and as I grew up it dawned on me that the world of men is a world of intractable hardship and I'd spend the rest of my life dealing with that reality.

❧

It was during that summer, in a narrow street paved with flagstones in the Old Town of Wangying, that a group came marching with martial solemnity. Father (and a few of his colleagues) walked at the head of the group wearing high glued-paper hats, while armed workers marched behind them shouldering spears and modern rifles. I had never seen Father dressed to look so comical before, and I ran home meaning to bring Grandmother out to share in the joke. On arrival, I saw tears in everyone's eyes. Grandmother enfolded me tightly in her arms lest calamity snatch away her grandson, too. I realized in a muddled way that perhaps something very bad had happened.

Immediately after, our home was raided and searched, and Grandmother's sewing machine was confiscated. For a while, a machine gun was set up pointed at our door to intimidate and humiliate us. My two sisters had to leave school, Father was constantly being paraded and beaten, and all over our door and windows they plastered large-character posters attacking Mother.

Grandmother watched over me anxiously, concerned that I would suffer discrimination and bullying. One day when the rebel faction came to excoriate Father, I cluelessly kept skylarking at the side of the room, and when they left he vented on me his long-suppressed rage. It was the first time he ever rained blows on me with a stick, and no one dared try to stop him in his fury. But Grandmother wrapped herself around me with a cry and the ring finger of her hand was broken when it took one of the blows of his stick. She endured this stoically and did not seek treatment. To the end of her life, that finger remained crooked. For my part, I never fully got over the trauma of that incident.

The campaign escalated relentlessly, and we could only wonder when our misfortunes would end. To help my older sister find a livelihood (for she could no longer attend school), Grandmother decided to go back to her old home on the plains and work the land, which would give my sister a chance to join the Production Brigade there. She thought her relatives and friends would make room for herself and her grandchild in troubled times. I was only five and no one had the heart to tell me she was leaving. Quietly she packed her simple bag, and each night she'd wipe away a tear as she hugged me, urging me for God's sake not to get in trouble outside, not to go swimming in the river, not to play with fire; and I sensed that something big must be happening, but all I could do was cry with her. When I awoke one morning and couldn't find my Grandma anywhere, I was inconsolable. Whether she tried explaining, or just slapped me, Mother could do nothing to change my heartbroken longing to bring Grandmother back. The world of my childhood had caved in.

After a year, my older sister went to cast her lot in with Grandmother in a village near a lake on the plains—the place was called Erwutai.[132] Second Sister took a job in the mines. Father was still being persecuted, but when the TB progressed to the stage of perforating his lungs, someone in the Coal Bureau stepped in to protect him and he was sent to Wuhan for treatment. Then my mother and I moved into a one-room apartment at the Grocery Co-Op, where life went steadily downhill. At her work unit, Mother was classified as 'a Rightist working under supervision for the purpose of being reformed,' which meant she had no time to take care of me. I wasted away and at night my coughing kept her awake. Alarmed, she took me into the city to be examined at the County Hospital, and when they gave me the same diagnosis as my father—perforating TB—she nearly fainted dead away. Back then, this was a fatal and contagious disease. She never gave up and did her best to conceal her tears from me: she spent everything she had on the drugs and injections that might snatch me from the Grim Reaper's hand.

There was no hope of surviving this disease without good nutrition and nursing. Mother had little choice but to write Grandmother a letter beseeching her to come back and take care of me. But it had been after suffering hard times in the hill country that Grandmother had gone home. She had struggled to build a safe and peaceful life for herself there and did not want to come back to this wretched place. After a while Eldest Sister wrote Mother: *Let Little Brother write Grannie himself, that's the only way she'll be persuaded to go back.* So I wrote her a letter. I was twelve, and I can't remember what I said, but years later Eldest Sister told me that Grandmother read it in tears. Every night she'd pull the letter from under her pillow, re-read it, and cry some more; and after a month, she decided to return to the hills to save the little one who, of all the people in her life, was most dear to her.

Mother had to go to Wanxian to pick her up at the wharf. The next day when I came home from school, I saw from a distance that the door of our house was ajar. I ran and burst in and found a fire in the hearth burning with a fragrant warmth that I had missed for a long time. Grandmother was there, catching up on the news with old Mrs. Kuang. I flung myself into her arms, wailing. Years of missing her and not being able to do anything about it changed instantly into a river of tears. I kept repeating, "Grannie! Grannie!" like some pitiable child dying in sight of his only kin. Grannie gently stroked my thin, small frame, her voice husky, and even Mrs. Kuang choked up. Grannie explained that to save money, Mama had let her come back on the first ride available; Mama would get a ride the following day.

Under the care of my mother and grandmother, the lesions in my lungs calcified and the same remarkably fortunate outcome occurred with my father. Once again, Grandmother had pulled our family back from the brink, and it was with the first stirrings of hope that we turned to face the year 1976.

∾

Grandmother was a cultured person to the marrow of her bones; it was a pity that she had been born into an old-fashioned family that saw little value in the education of girls. When furthermore her mother had died young and her father had gone abroad, there was no chance she would enjoy regular systematic schooling. Had things worked out differently, she might have become a female scholar of rare attainments. For years she kept up the habit of reading in the time she had to spare from her household chores. She could read all the books I brought home from college where I majored in liberal arts, and she took great pleasure in discussing them with me. She liked to practice calligraphy with a brush, too, when she had time, and if you had seen her perfectly straight and balanced characters you would have had trouble believing they came from the hand of an old woman with bound feet.

In my childhood home there were no books to speak of, but from families in town that had belonged to the former upper class I got my hands on some battered old volumes which I read surreptitiously. Whenever my parents found one of these books, they'd seize it and burn it and give me a scolding, because if anyone had discovered these "poisonous weeds" on one of the occasions when our home was raided and searched, it would have put the grown-ups in grave danger. But Grandmother stood up for me and was supportive of my reading all kinds of decadent books; she even helped me hide them. During the years I was a schoolboy, the received wisdom held that reading books was a waste of time, and there weren't even any college admission tests.[133] Intrigued by Grandmother's skill in cutting fabric to make clothes (she even knew how to make garments of fur), I sometimes tried to imitate her with scissors and chalk and asked her to teach me the tailor's craft. "You're a man," she responded with great seriousness, in a way she had never spoken to me before. "You shouldn't learn women's work." What, then (I asked her), should I learn? She said when I was old enough I could go study Law. Maybe she didn't completely understand what the Law was that her father had studied, but she believed there was a need for genuine Law to be upheld in this world.

My grandmother's decency and kindness were part of her make-up: I would say she had been born with the Buddha-nature. She felt no hatred for anyone; not for the husband who had abandoned her nor for the people who had persecuted our family. She was cordial and courteous to all. She never asked anyone's help, but when anyone sought her assistance she would do everything in her power. Everywhere she went, she won the respect of anyone she dealt with: even those who were at odds with my parents spoke highly of her character. To this day I have not met anyone who practiced universal love as she did, that is, spontaneously and from the heart. She often urged me to be reasonable, because she believed in a rational order of right and wrong that preserves the harmony of the universe. My father, upon whom dramatic vicissitudes had inflicted extraordinary humiliations, was all his life a choleric man who did not outwardly show any tender feeling and was feared by those around him, but he always respected Grandmother. When I was in high school, I liked to roughhouse with the workers at my father's depot, and when I once broke my ankle doing this, Father gave the worker a savage dressing-down. Grandmother, who never criticized her son-in-law, gently corrected him this time: "You shouldn't blame anyone else. It had to be the boy's own doing. There's no way any of the workers would have thrown your kid to hurt him." Seeing her point, Father nodded without a word. When Grandmother passed away, it was the only time I ever saw him break down and cry.

☙

Truth be told, I had much less feeling for my parents than for my grandmother. The early education of my mind and heart came entirely from her, and when my parents harshly rebuked me she would often intercede to reconcile or excuse, so that Mother used to say Grandmother was spoiling me. Whenever we had to part, the occasion invariably brought us to tears: even after I went to college in 1978 and would go back at the end of each vacation, she would always accompany me a good part of the way there and neither of us could help crying.

By that time I was grown, and in our home she had not only raised me and my two sisters but had done the same for three younger cousins of mine. She practiced extreme frugality, managing all household tasks herself and maintaining the old custom of not eating at the table with the rest of the family. Moreover, she regularly ate leftovers and refused to let anything go to waste. The family's economic condition improved steadily once the Cultural Revolution ended, but she would not soften the brutally Spartan way of life she had adopted in hard times, and my parents were often mortified that people might think they were abusing the old lady. For example, she would sneak downtown looking for scraps of junk that she could sell, or she would gather up the rotten leaves which farmers at the vegetable market peeled off their cabbages, bringing these home to clean them up and make something for herself to eat. As soon as we three kids had jobs we began giving her a little money, but she never spent a dime; she saved it to send to her young "mother-in-law." Mother never had anything good to say about that illiterate girl and, since she was now well cared-for in Fourth Great-Uncle's household, strenuously objected to Grandmother's sending her money. But Grandmother never forgot how, during the '30s, the mother-in-law had saved her life by lending her a few pounds of rice.

Mother was Grandma's only child, but in later years their relationship showed increasing strain. The principal sore point lay in their very different attitudes toward my grandfather. Mother loathed the father who had abandoned her and blighted her whole life with a political taint, while Grandmother met Mother's denunciations with a silence tinged with melancholy nostalgia. For example, when taking stock of me she'd sometimes sigh, "In this respect you're quite like your grandfather," and mother would bristle because she sensed the words were spoken more in praise than in blame.

By the time I was out on my own, Grandmother felt that she had completed her task in life and became extremely homesick, so that each time some disagreement arose with my mother she would blurt, "Let me go back to my home on the plains!" But Grandmother had only a few impoverished, distant relatives back there now, and mother was naturally unwilling to let her go. Later, when Eldest Sister was pregnant, she had Grandmother come to Wuhan to help her. But once that was taken care of, Grandmother slipped away with a relative of hers to the countryside near Hanchuan and made it clear she wasn't coming back. This relative was even older than she; the two had been like sisters to each other since their youth. In old age they now surprised everyone by leaving their families (full of children and grandchildren) and renting a room in a village, where Grandmother once more took up her needle and thread to earn their living. This occasioned much consternation in both families, but no one could change their minds or make them come back to town. We could think of little else: how hard it must be for these old women, all alone . . . and we were afraid we'd be reproached for neglect. We couldn't understand, then, what the old ladies really needed. The extended family agreed it was necessary for me to get on the case, so I made my way down to the plain. I arranged for older second cousins who were still working in Hanchuan to invite the two ladies to their home on some pretext. When I walked in, I became very emotional and knelt down in supplication; I really couldn't bear to let Grandmother suffer hardship in the countryside. I hugged her legs and wept. The tears began coursing down her cheeks. The relative who had been her companion wiped away a tear, too, and grumbled, "I knew you'd get wobbly if Ping'r showed up." Grandmother tried to lift me to my feet but I declared I would not stand up unless she was coming back with me. She was evidently conflicted but finally sighed, "All right, then, I'll go back with you." This is how I brought my grandmother back from her ancestral home to the hill country where she did not want to finish her life. It troubles me to think of this now. I denied an old woman's long-cherished wish: was that filial piety, or cruelty?

❧

After I started working, the need for frequent travel made parting with Grandmother become less and less an occasion for tears. In the autumn of 1983, Eldest Sister brought her little child back to the hill country for a joyful family visit. Needing to attend a meeting in a neighboring county, I said goodbye to Grandmother that morning, but she insisted on accompanying me downstairs, and suddenly I found myself choking back sobs, unable to speak. She, too, began to sob. At that moment I was struck by the stooped frailty of her spine and the white hair in disarray at her temples, and a nameless, boundless grief welled up, and the tears which I had not cried for some time flowed freely. What happened later convinced me that we have premonitions of death, though we cannot articulate them at the time.

Three days later I returned through Enshi, stopping to see my father, and he said, "I've been trying to reach you. Grandmother's in a bad way. She may not make it." We raced to Lichuan, and all during the drive I clung to the hope that she might pull through. I had never expected Death to come so suddenly; I had assumed I'd have time to say the things that needed to be said and find words to thank her for all her loving care. With this abrupt calamity I realized that it was too late.

When I rushed to her bedside with a cry, her mind still had a little lucidity but she was slurring her words. Bending close, I heard: "You've come, Ping'r? I'm all right. Don't cry. I just need to burp a little and then I should be fine . . ." Then I could no longer make out what she was murmuring. She did not open her eyes.

That morning Eldest Sister had planned to catch the bus back to Wuhan. Mama and Second Sister accompanied her to the bus stop, and Grandmother insisted on going with them, as if she sensed this might be the last time they'd see each other. Eldest Sister took her leave, wiping away a tear, and when the bus drove off, Grandmother turned back in haste. From behind, Second Sister noticed her gait becoming unsteady and when she ran to take her arm, Grandmother was on the point of keeling over. At the hospital they took one look, said it was a brain hemorrhage, and immediately listed her in critical condition.

At that time, this small-town hospital was primitively equipped and, having few specialists, they couldn't offer any effective treatment. I stood watch for ten days, never leaving her side, and observed with my own eyes the entire protracted process of her dying. The coma deepened until her pupils filled her irises; I cooled her with ice, rubbed her back, and suctioned her when she became congested. I wept and called out to her, convinced that she had not completely lost consciousness. At times tears filled her eyes and she breathed a sigh; and once, after I swore to her that I would take her back to her ancestral home, I distinctly felt her hand squeeze mine and shake it.

But the situation was irretrievable, and one morning she who had loved me more than anyone else in my life departed into the far distance. This had been inevitable, but it's still hard to accept it when a living person breathes her last as you hold her; you feel keenly then how frail and fragile is man. Who among us is a match for Death?

&

With my own hands I placed her in her coffin; with my own hands I dug her grave; and with my own hands I cast the first three shovelfuls of earth. I composed an inscription and wrote it with a brush upon the headstone for the mason to chisel. Then I built a sturdy concrete tomb. At first I had meant to take her back to be buried in her ancestral home, but hard are the roads of Shu;[134] too many difficulties barred the way, and my parents could not agree to it. There was nothing else to do but lay her to rest, for the time being, in a land that was not her own.

I could see her grave from my bedroom in the work unit's dorm. Many a melancholy evening I would walk over and sit quietly beside the tomb. Though solidly built, it developed a crack after two months. Thinking the stonemason hadn't sealed it properly, Mother bought some cement and had it repaired. But a few months later, the monument developed an even bigger fissure so that the headstone was on the point of toppling. I told my mother, "It shows Grandmother wants to go back where she came from." She was well aware of her mother's wish, but she couldn't do much about it now. On yellow tracing paper I wrote Grandmother a letter vowing that in ten years I would take her back to the plains, saying I hoped she could understand, and begging her to make no more cracks in her tomb. Kneeling before her grave, I burned the letter, and after I fixed the cement this time, there actually were no more cracks.

With Grandmother gone, I didn't feel like staying in the hill country. Within a year I was heading to the plains—as it happened, along the very road by which she had once come —and I kept going, and my road became rough . . . When I returned to the Ba Mountains ten years later, my father had died and my mother had gone missing, and I was an ex-con with nothing to my name. I had no way to repay those whom I had loved and lost, but I was determined to fulfill Grandmother's longstanding wish. I was going to break the tomb, open the coffin, gather up her bones and bear them on my back, if need be, down to the plains.

I had nailed together a wooden chest and brought a few friends with me into the hills. None of us had any experience with this sort of thing and we didn't know in what condition we might find a body that had been buried twelve years before. I knelt before the grave and wept as I burned paper for her, poured a libation, and lifted my eyes in prayer: "Grandma, if you want to come back to your homeland with me, it will help if you can be just a skeleton." Coffins were well-made in those days, and I didn't know what I would do if her body had remained intact: how could I move her then?

It would not be easy, given the long and difficult route.

Nervously my friends and I excavated the tomb and when the moment came to pry open the coffin, I couldn't watch. I stood to one side and waited for my friends to tell me what they found. When they removed the lid, the breeze wafted an unexpected scent of sandalwood. Only when a friend called, "No problem. Come take the bones," did I dare to look: in the coffin which had been perfectly intact, there was nothing left of Grandmother but a clean skeleton; her flesh and her clothes were completely gone. I gathered her bones carefully into the chest I had brought, and finally took her back to the plains, fulfilling my pledge to her and making some requital for all her kindness.

❧

Years later, I still wake in tears from unsettled dreams in which Grannie or my parents have appeared to me. When the dream dissolves and the tears have dried, I can't help thinking how fine it would be if there really were, somewhere outside the world we know, an underworld, a realm where the dead live on. In that other world, separated kinsmen might meet again, and death would hold no more terrors. Those who loved you are waiting at the next station down the line, and when you catch up with them you will all come together as a family again: any debts of love can then be paid, and everything can find redemption. A wondrous prospect! Even if you must needs relive all the destitution and squalor, the persecution and grief, you'll be together with those you loved most, never to be abandoned or separated again, no, never again: is there anything you could not then endure?

But death is a one-way ticket; no traveler returns with tidings of the other side. Loved ones who've gone before us seem to have broken faith; having drunk from the River Lethe, they may no longer remember us children left behind. It's hard to put credence in the communications we receive from them now and then in our dreams. There are countless religions that tell us what to think of death, but without an assurance of reunion with loved ones after the disasters of this life, what good are these religions to me, however much they promise well-being and success?

Many who knew my grandmother have sighed to me, "Such a good person!" Ah, but good people never have good lives—it's an unwritten rule of our wicked world. The good come into this world to suffer: like a grain of sugar cast into the sea, they cannot change its bitterness, and perhaps none but the passing fish shall ever know that trace of sweetness.

Each of us has his own story about a loving relative; and buried under every tombstone lies a long tale of cruel suffering. How can the gossamer of the written word bear the weight of that tale, honestly told? Yet if there is no Heaven to receive the souls of the dead, then let the writing of their story be a spiritual settling of accounts, to repay in this life the debts incurred in this life. What else can we do that will have any impact on the world?

Translator's Notes

1. *labeled a Rightist* In the latter half of 1957, shocked (or perhaps secretly pleased with the success of a trap—historians differ) by the extent of criticisms voiced at the invitation of his Hundred Flowers campaign, Mao branded the complainers "Rightists." The ensuing purge ended the careers (and in some cases the lives) of hundreds of thousands of distinguished intellectuals and administrators. The reader may find it curious that the author's mother, living in obscurity in the countryside, became a target in this high-level persecution of intellectuals. Many of Mao's campaigns, though their themes and propaganda were determined at the top, were implemented by replication: cadres summoned from around the country to observe pilot projects (试点) would go home to carry out the program and show cadres from still other locations what *they* needed to do. As a result, low-level cadres who were eager to prove their zeal or who welcomed a pretext to settle personal scores might carry out the most arbitrary punitive actions in the name of the Central Government's campaign. Numerical quotas for penalties, which first appeared in 1951 during the Campaign to Suppress Counterrevolutionaries, also contributed to this outcome.

2. *Whampoa.* The Whampoa Military Academy was founded in Guangzhou by Sun Yat-sen in 1924, with Chiang Kai-shek as its first commandant. A number of men who would make history in the war against Japan, the Civil War, and the early years of the People's Republic were either students or teachers at the academy in its first years. The eighth graduating class entered in 1930, by which time the academy had been moved to Nanjing.

3. *Enshi.* A prefecture comprising eight counties in southwestern Hubei. Since about half of the population belongs to the Tujia or Miao minority peoples, it is classified as an Autonomous Prefecture, the only one in Hubei. Enshi is also the name of the city which is the seat of the prefectural

government.

4. *Revolution U.* The abbreviated name of Hubei People's Revolution University, founded at Wuhan in 1949.

5. *knocked down.* His father was the Communist director of a mine. In the Cultural Revolution, it was typical for people in positions of responsibility to be relieved of their duties and subject to various forms of humiliation, even in the absence of ideological issues.

6. *1978.* Mao had died in 1976, and Deng Xiaoping was consolidating his pragmatic leadership even as he worked to undo some of the extremism of the Cultural Revolution.

7. *resigned from law enforcement and soon after went to prison* In June 1989 after the crackdown at Tiananmen, the author resigned in protest from his job as assistant to a police chief on Hainan. Thereafter he was active in circles that worked for political liberalization despite a climate of renewed repression. He was arrested in a sting when he agreed to relay a secret official document which he was told would be useful to the democracy movement, and he was imprisoned for four years.

8. *prickly ash tree.* The *Zanthoxylum Simulans.*

9. *Ping'r* This diminutive is an affectionate nickname for the author, whose given name is Shiping.

10. *the Code Enforcers.* A literal translation would be 'Urban Management'—the *chengguan* are low-level law-enforcement staff in every Chinese city, notorious for their brutality to street vendors.

11. *Yangluo, downstream from Wuhan.* The author's oldest sister lived on the right bank of the Yangtze in the Qingshan neighborhood of Wuhan, close to the steelmill. Yangluo Town is on the left bank, about eleven miles downstream, shortly after the river takes a turn to the right.

12. *surrendered her worn-out flesh as nourishment for the fish* In the Jatakas, an earlier incarnation of the Buddha is shown feeding himself to a hungry tigress out of compassion for her cubs, and the motif is familiar in cultures touched by

Buddhism.

13. *the key is on the windowsill.* Li Si's 1984 Chinese trans-
     lation is here rendered literally into English. Ginsberg
     quoted his mother thus: "The key is in the window, the
     key is in the sunlight at the window—I have the key—Get
     married Allen don't take drugs—the key is in the bars, in
     the sunlight in the window." Ginsberg's mother was in a
     psychiatric hospital with bars on the windows: the Chinese
     translation adapts her mystical revelation into a tangible,
     practical key which a mother has left on the windowsill for
     her son, and this is how it has become known to a genera-
     tion of Chinese readers.

14. *Great Well* The literal meaning of Da Shui Jing, a place
     name.

15. *ancestral hall* In this hall memorial tablets were displayed
     in honor of deceased ancestors, and ceremonies were held
     on certain days of the year.

16. *in order to complete a volume* The author was at that time
     employed in the Propaganda Department of Lichuan City.

17. *Liu Wencai* Liu Wencai was a landlord in Sichuan during
     the Republican period. Although he died shortly before
     the Communists took over Sichuan, the CCP used him
     for decades as a poster child for the exploitative cruelty of
     landlords under the old regime. After his manor had been
     made a museum, one of the courtyards was converted into
     a sculpture garden depicting the collection of rents from
     suffering peasants.

18. *the traditional Tujia style* The Tujia people are one of the
     two minority ethnic groups that are concentrated in the
     prefecture of western Hubei where the action of this story
     took place.

19. *marauding cultists* The late 1920s and early 1930s were a
     troubled era of weak central authority that saw the rise of
     local millennarian groups reminiscent of the larger nine-
     teenth-century movements known to history as the Taiping
     and the Boxers.

20. *marched to Yichang and took part in the battle there.* In May and June of 1940, the Chinese repulsed a Japanese attempt to seize the city of Yichang in preparation for an attack upriver on the Chinese seat of government in Chongqing.

21. *land-reform campaigns* As a nationwide, organized process, these ran from 1950 to 1953. Estimates of the number of landlords killed during this time range from slightly under a million to more than three million.

22. *a bad element* A formal classification during the Mao era, though it was applied flexibly to anyone suspected of disloyalty to the regime.

23. *Of the Three Gorges, long is the Wu at Badong* The sixth-century *Commentary on the Waterways Classic* is here quoting a fisherman's song. The Wu is the middle of the three gorges: it runs from Wushan in Chongqing (until 1997 considered part of Sichuan) down to Badong in Hubei, and is not in fact the longest of the three. The enormity known to the world as the Three Gorges Dam was built farther down the Yangtze in the last of the three gorges.

24. *Eight li from Flagstone Village* The traditional *li* (里) has been standardized at half a kilometer, or about one-third of a mile, but in earlier times and especially in mountainous terrain it often measured a shorter distance. The Wikipedia entry cites a WWII memoir to suggest that "It could be longer or shorter depending on the effort required to cover the distance."

25. *They knew naught of the Han* An allusion to Tao Qian's *Tale of the Peach-Blossom Spring*, the fable of an isolated community cut off from the world.

26. *The Government began to exercise more direct control over them* The author is referring to an Imperial policy known as 改土归流 (*gai tu gui liu*) under which local hereditary chieftains who had been set over minority communities during the Yuan Dynasty were replaced with appointed

officials usually of Han ethnicity. The policy was implemented in various frontier regions at different times: commencing during the Ming, it was completed under the Qing thanks to the systematic impetus of the Emperor Yongzheng in the first half of the eighteenth century.

27. *they were vague on the distinction between the Ba and the Chu.* This is understandable, as both belong to ancient history. The Ba were absorbed into the Qin empire in 316 B.C.E. The Chu people who were their powerful frenemies to the east fell to the Qin about 90 years later. The area around Flagstone passed from the control of Ba to that of Chu sometime in the fifth century B.C.E.

28. *Lin Yaohua's . . . The Golden Wing* This influential work from the 1940s is available online in English at http://archive.org/details/goldenwingsociol00liny.

29. *To sing of the bamboo and the willow* Referring to two genres of ancient folk songs that originated before the Tang Dynasty but were popularized by the use which Bai Juyi and Wen Tingyun made of the form. The "bamboo branch songs" are quatrains typically grounded in the experience of everyday life and are said to have originated in eastern Sichuan.

30. *The Guangxu Emperor* The next-to-last emperor of China, whose reign nominally ran from 1875 to 1908, though the Empress Dowager Cixi exercised true power during much of that time.

31. *his own militia* The word for 'militia' is historically specific, the 民团 organized by a landlord to protect his estate in that period of weak government.

32. *He Long's assault* He Long was a swashbuckling military man who started as an outlaw (after killing a tax-collector), formed his own personal army in Hunan, served the KMT during the Northern Expedition, then joined the Communists in 1927. He led a division of the Eighth Route Army in the last years of the 1930s, when he suppressed KMT-sympathizers in Hubei.

33. *four hectares* ten acres

34. *Governing by not doing* The 'not doing' is *wu wei*, one of the cardinal principles of Daoism.

35. *Hired a farmhand* The 长工 *changgong* of pre-Communist society was a kind of family retainer who helped work the fields.

36. *Long life brings many humiliations*: from the dialogue between Yao and the border guard in the "Heaven and Earth" chapter of the *Zhuangzi*.

37. *the great drive to "eliminate the bandits"* Especially in reference to the first years of Communist rule, the word "bandit" was consistently used in the official history where "insurgent" or "KMT holdout" would have been more accurate.

38. *Nowhere . . . is there land that does not belong to the King.* From the ancient poem 北山 *Bei Shan* in the *Book of Odes*.

39. *Cultivated by military garrisons to feed themselves* As in Note #26, the author is referring to a specific Imperial policy, in this case 屯田 (*tuntian*), whereby Han soldiers were sent into the border regions where they would farm tracts of land to support themselves. The practice occurred in tandem with *gai tu gui liu*.

40. *Tax-exemption on 15 mu* In the Ming Dynasty, the *mu* was 0.14 acres; the size of this measure of area was slightly increased in the Qing and again in the Republican era. "Popular wisdom had it that it required 4 mu of land (about two-thirds of an acre) to feed one person." (Elliott, Mark C. *Emperor Qianlong: Son of Heaven, Man of the World*, p. 148. Longman: Upper Saddle River, 2009)

41. *Single-Whip Law . . . From Poll Tax to Land Tax* These were two programs of tax reform implemented, respectively, in the sixteenth century under the Ming and in the eighteenth century under the Qing. The first is 一条鞭 (though the *bian* is sometimes written with other characters) and the second is 摊丁入亩.

42. *Raising an opium crop* In the early 1940s, the Party sup-

ported itself in the northern base areas by selling opium to areas under KMT control. Of this product, some the Party had planted (as Ye Fu says), but much was smuggled in from areas under Japanese control. See Chen, Yungfa, "The Blooming Poppy Under the Red Sun: The Yan'an Way and the Opium Trade" in Saich, Tony, and Hans J. van de Ven (eds.) *New Perspectives on the Chinese Communist Revolution* p. 263ff. M. E. Sharpe 1997. This history is easily forgotten because in the 1950s Mao energetically and effectively shut down the opium trade. Since the imposition of the drug by the British in the nineteenth century remains one of the chief grievances nursed by the Party, Mao's profiting from the odious business is a sensitive subject.

43. *As Lu Xun once said . . .* In the 1933 essay "A year of *Analects*" clashing with Lin Yutang on the place of humor in Chinese life.

44. *Abdication in primordial times* The legendary emperors Yao and Shun (late 3rd millennium B.C.E.) are said to have ceded their thrones to chosen and worthy successors.

45. *Mirror of Governance* The 资治通鉴, a massive (294 volumes) and meticulous work of history produced in the eleventh century by Sima Guang.

46. *The Xinhai Revolution* deposed the Qing Dynasty in 1911 and ushered in the Republican era.

47. *The Tatars* In the West, this term (sometimes rendered "Tartar") designates the Mongols or the Turkic people who swept across Asia to the southeastern corner of Europe. But in China, the Jurchen (from whom the Manchu descended) are sometimes called the Jurchen/Ruzhen Tatars.

48. *Though a man of Chu might lose his axe* An epigram attributed to the King of Chu and first recorded by Gongsun Long of the Warring States period. In its original form it referred to a bow, not an axe: when on a hunting expedition the King misplaced his bow, he told his servants with these words not to search for it. Though variously interpreted and applied over time, it seems to express both

equanimity and a communal sense of welfare.

49. *Labor camp at Shayang* Later named a Re-education Through Labor center, this camp in central Hubei was still being cited in the early years of the 21st century in connection with the alleged torture of Falun Gong practitioners. It lies in an agricultural district beside the Han River.

50. *Mutual-aid groups* These were small coöperative groups (of approximately ten households) which shared draft animals and practiced a more specialized division of labor than was possible on single-family farms. Mao called for them in 1951; their adoption was for the most part voluntary and often yielded good results (See Ralph A. Thaxton, Jr, *Catastrophe and Contention in Rural China*, CUP 2008, p. 90ff) *Coöperatives* These were larger groups that pooled land and divided the harvest according to varying principles. The practice was strongly promoted from Beijing starting in or before 1952, according to Thaxton. *People's Communes* A signature (and ruinous) innovation of the Great Leap Forward, collectivizing not only agricultural production but also cooking and dining in communes of up to ten thousand families.

51. *The three rural problems* Alluding to a letter addressed to Premier Zhu Rongji in March 2000 by Li Changping, then a low-level Party Secretary in Hubei, that said: "Peasants are really poor, rural life is extremely hard, and agriculture is in real crisis." The background is explained in remarks by Dr. Lei Guang at a 2006 conference at the University of Chicago, http://chicagosociety.uchicago.edu/china/coverage/PoliticsPanel.pdf. The publication of this letter by *Southern Weekend* made Li and his words famous.

52. *Treated as an enlightened country gentleman* In the parlance of the CCP, "enlightened" meant "associated with the old order but not hostile to the Party, and therefore not to be treated as a foe."

53. *December 9* On December 9, 1935, thousands of university students in Beijing took to the streets to demand that

the KMT stop making concessions to the Japanese invaders who were expanding their control of northeast China. Yao Yilin (1917-1994) was among the Communist organizers of that demonstration. See also Note #58.

54. *Alliance for National Salvation* The 牺盟会, an abbreviation which if fully unpacked would mean Alliance of Those Willing to Sacrifice Themselves to Save the Nation. It was initially a joint effort of the CCP and KMT but slid under Communist control, training troops that distinguished themselves in the war against Japan.

55. *Mentioned together with Li Dingming and Liu Shaobai* Li Dingming (1881-1947) was a learned practitioner of Chinese medicine who treated Mao and enjoyed a relationship of mutual respect with him. Never a Party member, in the 1930s he was prominent in representative government in a district not far from Yan'an and was held in honor by the local gentry. Liu Shaobai (1883-1968) was also a member of the gentry who in 1905 had scored high in the last Imperial examinations, but he had pronounced Leftist sympathies. In 1930 he rented part of the mansion of Ji Xiaolan in Beijing and sheltered Communist operatives in it; this building has been preserved as a museum. In 1937 Liu secretly joined the Party and after 1949 would serve in the CPPCC.

56. *liberated areas.* The Communists' term for districts under their control during the Civil War.

57. *Like an ox on parade* A cruel pun: the family name Niu means "ox" or "cow."

58. *Yao Yilin* joined the Party in 1935 and rose to high offices including the Vice Premiership. In 1989 he was one of the hardliners who pushed for a crackdown on the students in Tiananmen Square. He died in 1994. His memoir, edited from a series of talks he delivered in the mid-1980s, was published in 2008.

59. *The people should count for more than the sovereign* 民重君 轻 is a simplification of the maxim of Mencius (Jin Xin II,

No. 60) 民為貴, 社稷次之, 君為輕. "The people are the most important element in a nation; the spirits of the land and grain are the next; the sovereign is the lightest." (Transl. Legge)

60. *Sun Wukong: "Emperors take turns..."* From the dialogue between the Monkey King and the Buddha in Chapter 7 of *Journey To the West*. Sun Wukong proposes to dethrone the Jade Emperor from his celestial palace.

61. *Hong Xiuquan*, who launched the Taiping Rebellion which convulsed China for fifteen years in the middle of the 19th century, established his capital at Nanjing, which he named Tianjing ('Heavenly Capital').

62. *When Engels addressed the land question . . .* "As soon as our Party is in possession of political power, it has simply to expropriate the big landed proprietors, just like the manufacturers in industry. Whether this expropriation is to be compensated for or not will, to a great extent, depend not upon us but the circumstances under which we obtain power, and particularly upon the attitude adopted by these gentry, the big landowners, themselves. We by no means consider compensation as impermissible in any event; Marx told me (and how many times!) that, in his opinion, we would get off cheapest if we could buy out the whole lot of them." Friedrich Engels, *The Peasant Question in France and Germany* (Chapter 2: Germany) available online at https://www.marxists.org/archive/marx/works/1894/peasant-question/ch02.htm Ye Fu's addition "and distribute it to the poor" may need to be qualified. From the same work by Engels: "The main point is, and will be, to make the peasants understand that we can preserve their houses and fields for them only by transforming them into co-operative property operated co-operatively."

63. *The First Party Congress* convened at Shanghai in the summer of 1921.

64. *Most . . . chose to resign.* Exactly half of them resigned, and of these six, one rejoined the Party in 1949, one left

in 1938 because he lost out in a struggle for primacy with Mao Zedong, and two would later serve in the Japanese puppet government at Nanjing and be tried for treason. Revulsion over the criminality of the CCP does not seem, therefore, to have been the dominant motive in most of the resignations.

65. *The ideal of the Three Principles of the People.* Referring to Sun Yat-sen's slogan of "Nationalism, Democracy, and Social Welfare" in which each term contains the character for "people" (民族主义, 民权主义, 民生主义).

66. *The May 21 incident* (马日事变), sometimes translated very literally as "Horse-Day Incident," was a night of bloodletting in Changsha when a detachment of the National Army attacked the offices of the CCP and allied organizations. This turning-point passed largely unnoticed in the West, perhaps because it happened a few hours before Lindbergh landed in Paris.

67. *An armed uprising* In the late summer and early fall of 1927 the Communists launched two uprisings in Jiangxi and Hunan. Both were put down. The Communist fighters withdrew into the Jingang Mountains between the two provinces and reorganized on the basis of simple disciplinary rules, written by Mao, that are widely believed to have contributed significantly to the triumph of Communist arms in the Civil War: "(1) Obey orders in all your actions. (2) Don't take a single needle or piece of thread from the masses. (3) Turn in everything captured."

68. *Tsarist Russia practiced a village commune system.* (村社制度) In the Russian language, it was called the Obshchina (община) or Mir (мир) —basically, a peasant commune. It did indeed conduct periodic redistribution of land and formed an important part of Russia's social structure between the emancipation of the serfs in 1861 and the agrarian reforms of 1906. Prior to emancipation, the *obshchina* functioned as an intermediary between the landlord and the peasants; to some extent it did so even after emancipa-

tion, because most of the peasants had to compensate their former lord for the land granted them along with their freedom, and the *obshchina* managed these "redemption obligations." The historical literature is extensive: for a concise but detailed treatment, see Francis M. Watters, "The Peasant and the Village Commune," in Vucinich, Wayne S., and John Shelton Curtiss (ed.s), *The Peasant in 19th-Century Russia*, Stanford, 1968.

69. *Land reform on Taiwan* The process had several stages culminating in the 1953 "Land to the Tiller" act, which by the following year had transferred ownership of almost 350,000 acres of land to almost 200,000 farmers who had until then been tenants. One of the architects of the program, Chen Cheng, described the program in his 1961 book *Land Reform in Taiwan*. At http://markweatherall. wordpress.com/2010/06/17/land_reform_in_taiwan/, Mark Weatherall summarizes the history and offers a look at the methods used to finance the land purchases.

70. *At age four* The author was born in 1962. The Cultural Revolution began in the summer of 1966.

71. *A hack writer invented . . .* Huang Shiren was the villainous landlord in *The White-Haired Girl*, a 1945 opera by Yan Jinxuan that would be adapted into one of the Eight Model Works that dominated the performance arts of the Cultural Revolution. Nan Batian was the tyrannical landlord in *The Red Detachment of Women*, a 1961 film for which Liang Xin wrote the screenplay in 1958. (It found favor with Zhou Enlai and with his encouragement in 1964 was made into a ballet which became one of the other Eight Model Works). Zhou Bapi was the antagonist in a vignette appearing in the 1951 autobiographical novel *Gao Yubao*. This little tale of a landlord who mimics the crowing of a rooster at midnight in order to make his peasants rise early to toil for him was later edited into a short story included in schoolbooks nationwide, and in 1964 it was made into the animated film *A Cock Crows at Midnight*

(半夜鸡叫).

72. *For class struggle to remain the focus of discussion day after day, month after month . . .* Paraphrasing an exhortation of Mao Zedong uttered at the Tenth Plenum of the Central Committee, in September 1962.

73. *The Truth About Liu Wencai* 《刘文彩真相》 by Xiao Shu, published in 1999 by Shaanxi Normal University Press and subsequently withdrawn from sale.

74. *The inscription read* The epitaph is written in classical Chinese. Though few can write this way today, most readers can understand it or at least get the gist of it.

75. *In the twenty-sixth year* The text uses an archaic, formal calendar based on a 60-year cycle. The year referred to was 1949.

76. *That famous period of ten years* The Cultural Revolution, 1966-76.

77. *1976* The year of Mao's death.

78. *the return of the capitalist-roader* Deng Xiaoping made two comebacks from an official obloquy tantamount to banishment.

79. *Zhang Zhixin* A staunch Party member whose criticisms of Jiang Qing, Lin Biao, and Mao himself early in the Cultural Revolution led to her arrest in 1969, followed by six years of maltreatment in a Liaoning prison. In April 1975 she was impaled and decapitated; some accounts say that in preparation for her execution her larynx was slashed lest she make a statement on the execution ground.

80. *The gentleman stays far from the kitchen* From the *Mencius,* Book 1, Part 1, Chapter 7: "So is the superior man affected towards animals, that, having seen them alive, he cannot bear to see them die; having heard their dying cries, he cannot bear to eat their flesh. Therefore he keeps away from his slaughter-house and cook-room." (Transl. Legge)

81. *Li Zicheng and Hong Xiuquan* Leaders of violent nationwide revolts in the seventeenth and nineteenth centuries, respectively. That they were responsible for the deaths of

millions makes it all the more relevant that Mao admired them and that they are depicted with respect in modern pop culture.

82. *Uprising of the Three Townships* See p. 55.
83. *"An act of violence."* The "parallel sentences" to which the author refers form a celebrated passage in Mao's 1927 *Report on an Investigation of the Peasant Movement in Hunan*: "A revolution is not a dinner party, or writing an essay, or painting a picture, or doing embroidery. It cannot be so refined, so leisurely and gentle, so temperate, kind, courteous, restrained and magnanimous. A revolution is an insurrection, an act of violence by which one class overthrows another."
84. *Milan Kundera says . . .* See *The Unbearable Lightness of Being*, II.27 (p. 75 in the Harper & Row edition) "In spite of their love, they had made each other's life a hell." (Transl. Heim)
85. *Rectification of Styles:* Mao's campaign to purge some of the Communist intellectuals at Yan'an in a climate that came to resemble a witch-hunt. Especially in its final phase during 1943-44, there were forced public confessions of error, daily self-criticism, and accusations which led to the death of thousands of Party members. The campaign instilled a lasting insecurity in Chinese intellectuals and cemented Mao's dominance.
86. From a propaganda song *A folk song for the Party to hear: comparing the Party to my mother* (唱支山歌给党听，我把党来比母亲) associated with the 1962 "Learn from Lei Feng" campaign. Words by Yao Xiaozhou (1958).
87. *castanets* The Chinese 云板 *yunban*, made from two pieces of bamboo and associated in Daoist iconography with Cao Guojiu (Ts'ao Kuo-ch'iu), who was inducted into the Eight Immortals after saying that heaven was in his heart.
88. *Little Furball* 毛弟, 'younger brother Mao.' Mao here is an affectionate *given* name (not Mao Zedong's surname) evoking an animal's fur with the deliberate modesty with

166

which peasants nicknamed their children in order to avoid tempting Fate.

89. *A picked-up kid* 抱到儿 *baodao'r*, an expression that sounds odd in Mandarin and was apparently a dialect term used in Hubei.

90. *Zhang Zhidong* From 1889 to 1907 as Governor-General of Huguang (comprising Hubei and Hunan), shortly before the collapse of the Qing Dynasty, Zhang took steps to modernize both the army and the education system of the Empire. He also promoted commercial development as "trade war" (商战) in competition with European powers.

91. *Traditions about the eremitical life* In contrast with the Western tradition, Chinese motives for living in seclusion have been predominantly secular. An almost constant theme in Chinese tales of seclusion is the hermit's refusal to serve the Emperor as an official. A monograph by Alan J. Berkowitz, *Patterns of Disengagement: the practice and portrayal of reclusion in early medieval China* (Stanford University Press, 2000) provides extensive background on this cultural theme, enumerating the vocabulary of reclusion (p. xii) and a variety of eremitical archetypes (pp. 17-63). He includes a detailed treatment (p. 209-226) of Tao Hongjing, the Daoist hermit quoted near the end of this essay, and Tao Qian, the poet whose subjects of praise (the simple life, independence of spirit, and wine drunk in abundance) reverberate in the portrait of Su Jiaqiao.

92. *The greatest hermits* This aphorism is extant in a variety of forms, and goes back at least to the poem "The Middle Kind of Hermit" (中隐) by the Tang Dynasty poet Bai Juyi.

93. *The 'Treading' hexagram of the I Ching.* The reader intrigued by this allusion may study the tenth hexagram in that ancient book of divination, especially the interpretation of a changing line in the second position, since that is where the term 幽人 *youren* ('a man apart, a man of seclusion') occurs. Unfortunately, the standard Wilhelm-Baynes

translation provides a questionable rendering of 幽人 here and obscures the connection which Ye Fu is drawing. The James Legge version (available online at http://www. sacred-texts.com/ich/ic10.htm) is better for this purpose. The presence of a nine in the second position would lead dynamically, according to the logic of the *I Ching*, to the 25th hexagram, Guilelessness, which Legge glosses as having as its subject "one who is entirely simple and sincere." This, too, seems appropriate for Su Jiaqiao.

94. *Kong Yingda* A seventh-century Confucian commentator on the I Ching.

95. *The Nationalities colleges* Several regions in China have institutions of higher learning tailored for minority ethnic groups. The author and Su Jiaqiao attended the South Central College for Nationalities (中南民族学院) in Wu- han. In 2002, this college was upgraded to a university.

96. *I pushed away the pine; "Be off with you!"* The last line of Xin Qiji's Song Dynasty poem 西江月 · 遣兴, in which the inebriated poet thinks a pine tree is trying to help him stand up; protesting that he is not drunk, the poet pushes the tree away.

97. *We're not our skin of grime* From the last stanza of Gins- berg's 1955 "Sunflower Sutra": *We're not our skin of grime, we're not dread bleak dusty imageless locomotives, we're golden sunflowers inside, blessed by our own seed [. . .]*

98. *Feng Gong* (冯巩) a movie actor and well-known practitio- ner of the comedic form known as "crosstalk."

99. *The worthies of the Bamboo Grove* Seven literary or ar- tistic figures of the third century C.E. who, according to tradition, withdrew from the world of the Court into an informal society of bibulous intellectuals.

100. *Liu Baiyu, Wei Wei, and Yang Shuo* Three prominent prose writers of the '50s and '60s. Most of what they wrote would be considered arrant propaganda today, though they were not without skill as writers. Yang Shuo was driven to suicide during the Cultural Revolution. The other two

lived into the twenty-first century.

101. *Cut the mimeograph* In the West, xerographic photocopy-ing began replacing mimeography during the 1960s, but the older technology thrived for three more decades in China. One would spread wax paper on a steel plate whose surface had been roughened into countless tiny sharp bumps; writing with a stylus, one thus cut (with the strokes of the characters) thousands of tiny holes into the wax paper. Placed between a sheet of blank paper and an inked plate or drum, the wax paper became a stencil from which one or two hundred copies could be made before it wore out.

102. *The Jixia Academy* An institute of higher learning founded in the fourth century B.C.E. (not long after Plato estab-lished his Academy) within the territory of what today is Shandong Province. It was notable because, though privately run, it was founded and supported by a king, thus representing a very early (perhaps the first) instance of state-sponsored higher education, and because philoso-phers of contrasting traditions (and drawn from different Chinese states) taught and debated there. Sections of the *Mencius* appear to record discussions that occurred while Mencius was in residence at the academy. In older English texts it is sometimes called the "Academy of the Gate of Chi."

103. *A Tujia corpse-driver* In folk beliefs of northern Hunan and western Hubei as recorded by Shen Congwen, the corpse-driver (赶尸) was a sorcerer who could be hired to raise the bodies of those who had died far from their ancestral homes and conduct them to the place proper for their burial. People actually practicing this profession employed various means to lend to the corpses they carried an appearance of walking under their own power. Both in the folk legend and in the historical practice, these journeys were made late at night. When the author was a boy he often heard his elders speak of the phenomenon. Liao Yiwu

recounts the experience of one of the last of the corpse-drivers in a tale translated by Wen Huang as *The Corpse Walker.*

104. *a flowering of associations devoted to the New Literature* The literature that blossomed in the freer climate of the 1980s was called the New Literature in an echo of the "New Culture" promoted from 1915 to 1925.

105. *No background checks* The original 无须档案户口 refers to two specific means of personnel control: the dossier, a lifelong file recording incidents and evaluations at all an individual's work assignments, and the household registration, a certificate of legal residency without which it would have been difficult to obtain a monthly food ration.

106. *To head west, out through the sunny pass.* A phrase from a Tang Dynasty quatrain by Wang Wei (送元二使安西, "Seeing Yuan'er off on a mission to Anxi") that inspired a melancholy song of enduring popularity. The *Yangguan* ('sunny pass') is a fortified gate of the Great Wall in Gansu Province, and for centuries it marked the western edge of China.

107. *'Passing his own door'* Alluding to the legendary Yu the Great, who devoted himself so single-mindedly to his duties of flood control that when work took him through his own town he did not stop to visit his family.

108. *As sure as the thousand fathoms of Peach Blossom Pond* Alluding to a poem (李白乘舟将欲行) by Li Bai acknowledging, at their parting, the deep friendship shown him by Wang Lun.

109. *struggle sessions* Public and often violent efforts to break an individual's will by having a mob accuse him in what was, ostensibly, an effort to help him see and admit the error of his ways. Though typical of the Cultural Revolution, the struggle session long preceded it. There are conflicting opinions as to whether the practice reflects Russian influence. Priestland stresses the role of public "self-criticism" in the CPSU and says that, though initially resisted by

Chinese sensitive to "face," struggle sessions were "exported" from the Soviet Union to China (Priestland, David, *The Red Flag: A History of Communism*, Grove Press, 2009: p. 145-6). But Oleg Kharkhordin points out that in the Communist Party of the Soviet Union self-criticism (*samokritika*) usually denoted the Party's criticism of itself, and in practice that meant some individuals criticizing the deeds of of others (*The Collective and the Individual in Russia: A Study of Practices*, University of California Press, 1999: p. 145). He believes that Western observers erroneously imputed a Chinese phenomenon to the culture of Russian Communism: "...As a rule this type of individual confession was not practiced at Party or *kollectiv* meetings in the Soviet Union. Of course, people were often required to give self-accounts in public in front of Party assemblies or purge gatherings, but nobody expected that they should incriminate themselves. The misleading view that attributes confessions of individual faults to Russian Communists may come from the uncritical extension of the patterns demonstrated during the Cultural Revolution in China" (Kharkhordin 145). In an account that perhaps offers a way to reconcile these viewpoints, Jane L. Price relates the experience of the first generation of Chinese Communists to be trained in the Soviet Union. In 1927-1928 they were caught up in the struggle between Stalin and Trotsky, and since some of them inclined toward Trotsky, the Moscow branch of the CPSU conducted a purge of the Chinese students in a crackdown of unprecedented severity. " . . . [P]urge commissars descended upon the campus. They suspended classes and divided the student body into small groups for interrogation. . . . The CPSU branch at the University employed [a coterie of Chinese students loyal to Stalin] to hurl accusations against suspected Trotskyites and other anti-Party elements. One participant described the meetings as *shattering experiences for the individuals being scrutinized, for the slightest pos-*

sible blemish from the past was apt to be publicly questioned. Even one's family history going back to remote ancestors was thoroughly investigated. . . . [M]any of the weak people simply broke down. Even the most robust and strong-willed among us were bathed in their own sweat at these inquisitions. ... The entire "purification" process lasted three months. It was supervised by a Party Purge Committee headed by General Pavel Ivanovich Berzin, chief of intelligence for the Red Army General Staff." (pp. 95-96 of Price, Jane L., *Cadres, Commanders, and Commissars: the Training of the Chinese Communist Leadership, 1920 - 45*, Westview Press, 1976) The participant quoted is Sheng Yüeh, whose memoir Price commends as a record of the era (Sheng, Yüeh, *Sun Yat-sen University in Moscow and the Chinese Revolution: a Personal Account* (University of Kansas Center for East Asian Studies, 1971). Price adds that the coterie of loyal Chinese Bolshevists who were favored in this purge, and who enthusiastically "hurled accusations," became influential within the CPC upon their return to China. Later she mentions that this very group, now stigmatized as "formalists," was one of the prime targets of Mao's Rectification campaign in 1942, when struggle sessions were used intensively (Price 175). One might therefore speculate that though the struggle session exemplified Communism with Chinese characteristics, it was the fruit of an intervention in Moscow, ruthless and malignant even by Stalinist standards, that proved formative for the young CPC.

110. *The "angry right-wingers" of their day* The author uses a term (右愤, *youfen*) that came into online use during the first decade of the twentieth-first century to describe indignant critics of the Communist Party in contrast with its indignant defenders (who are known as 左愤 *zuofen*, 'angry left-wingers,' or, if young men, as 愤青 *fenqing* 'angry youths').

111. *Both found themselves unemployed* In a personal communication, the author recalled that this happened in the late 1980s. The "plant" was a Lichuan distillery that produced

corn liquor.

112. *Zhang Han* (张翰) A scholar and poet of the Western Jin Dynasty (late 3rd – early 4th centuries).

113. *Zhuangzi says . . .* Alluding to the celebrated Chapter 20 about the mountain tree. The author seems to compress into a single tree metaphor the lesson which Zhuangzi divided into two object lessons involving a tree and a goose.

114. *were to him no more than clouds floating past* An allusion to the *Analects* 7.6: "The Master said, 'With coarse rice to eat, with water to drink, and my bended arm for a pillow;—I have still joy in the midst of these things. Riches and honors acquired by unrighteousness, are to me as a floating cloud.'" (Transl. Legge)

115. *Shicun* The independent writer Yu Shicun has published bestsellers such as *Extraordinary Words* and was one of the first to sign Charter '08. *Qing Cheng* is the screen name of an internet commentator who is a judge in a local court.

116. *Feng Zikai* An artist, educator, and essayist who lived from 1898 to 1975 and is particularly remembered on account of the books he wrote and illustrated for children.

117. *Nie Gannu* Like Lu Xun, a member of the League of Left-Wing Writers in the 1930s; still admired for his poetry as well as his essays. He was imprisoned during the Cultural Revolution after a close friend, himself an esteemed calligrapher, informed on him. *Yang Xianyi* A literary translator who, in collaboration with his British wife, translated many classic works into English. His obituary in the *Telegraph* mentions that during the Campaign Against Spiritual Pollution, he would sometimes pick up his phone (which he believed to be tapped) and ask, "Where shall we go and get polluted tonight?"

118. *The meter of a Song-Dynasty lyric* The original is specific: Su Jiaqiao not only composed his message in the dense idioms of classical Chinese, but made it fit the tune *He Xin Liang*, "Welcoming the Start of Cool Weather." The form has two sections of 57 and 59 syllables, with phrases of different

but prescribed lengths and rhymes at prescribed intervals. I have not tried to reproduce this virtuosity in English.

119. *Du Fu* Widely considered one of the two greatest poets of the Tang Dynasty. The original uses a nickname, *Du Lang.*

120. *But now he says he likes Hu Shih better.* The point of this comparison of two cultural titans may be that where Lu Xun was generally content to satirize his world, Hu Shih engaged it with constructive intent. The vision motivating his remarkable career (he was at different times the best-known proponent of vernacular literature, an ambassador to the United States, and Chancellor of Beijing University) may perhaps be traced to John Dewey, who was his mentor when he earned his Ph.D. at Columbia.

121. *Weibo* An abbreviation for "micro-blog," the name of a popular social-media application combining features of Twitter and Facebook, where personal experiences are shared and current events commented on.

122. *What's in the hills? . . .* Tao Hongjing was a master of eso-teric Daoism who lived 456 – 536 C.E. and served as an able courtier in his youth. The title of this quatrain identi-fies it as a response to an inquiry from the Emperor Wu of the new Liang Dynasty, asking "What is in the hills?"—presumably, hoping to persuade Tao to leave his seclusion and return to service at Court. In saying he cannot take the white clouds in his hands and present them as a gift to His Majesty, Tao Hongjing may mean that the values of the Way cannot be grasped by the worldly-minded.

123. *Can any see the hermit passing by . . .* From a *ci* to the tune of *Bu Suan Zi* and beginning 缺月挂疏桐，漏断人初静.

124. *called her Brother Fenglin* In a personal communication, the author explained that it was a local custom of Han-chuan to address a virtuous eldest daughter (贤德的长女) as if she were the eldest son.

125. *Lingyun* The name means "Soaring to the clouds."

126. *Qiu Qingquan* (1902–49) A KMT general who had taken part in the Northern Expedition and who committed

suicide when he lost the key battle of Xubeng in the Civil War.

127. *Wanxian* In 1998 this town was renamed to Wanzhou and is part of the Chongqing provincial-level municipality.

128. *the time that would be called the three years of "natural disasters."* The Great Famine of 1958–62, caused by mismanagement of agriculture during the Great Leap Forward. See Yang Jisheng, *Tombstone*, FSG 2012.

129. *Ironworks . . . after using up all the local timber* The use of wood as fuel instead of hotter-burning coal was typical of the ill-conceived efforts to ramp up steel production during the Great Leap Forward.

130. *The Twenty-four Paragons* A fourteenth-century collection of edifying tales replete with outré examples of self-sacrificing filial devotion.

131. *Qualified for welfare* Specifically, the 五保户, a guarantee of food, shelter, medical care, clothing, and burial which was reserved in the Mao era for the childless and destitute aged of the countryside. Initiated in 1956, the program underwent repeated revision to reflect changing circumstances but in one form or another it lasted for fifty years.

132. *the place was called Erwutai* It is known today as Liudian Village (刘店村), about two miles southeast of Huadian Lake.

133. *reading books was a waste of time* During the Cultural Revolution, higher education basically shut down. This was not merely the institutional cost of conducting a vast, tumultuous, and all-consuming campaign. It reflected a value-judgment in favor of revolutionary violence and against the life of the mind, overturning not only millennia of Chinese respect for scholarship but even the "Red and Expert" ideal of the 1950s.

134. *Hard are the roads of Shu* Alluding to Li Bai's poem 蜀道难 describing the toilsome mountain roads of Sichuan.

LITTERA SCRIPTA MANET,
LECTA VIVIT,
DISSERTA MOVET

Ragged Banner Press depends on word-of-mouth advertising by satisfied readers. If you found this book of value, please tell your friends—and your librarian.

For orders, corrections, and further information, visit

http://www.raggedbanner.com